CIVIL RIGHTS MOVEMENT

Backlash: Race Riots in the Jim Crow Era

CIVIL RIGHTS MOVEMENT

Backlash: Race Riots in the Jim Crow Era

Calvin Craig Miller

MORGAN REYNOLDS
PUBLISHING

Greensboro, North Carolina

Civil Rights Movement
Backlash: Race Riots in the Jim Crow Era
Copyright © 2012 by Morgan Reynolds Publishing

Library of Congress Cataloging-in-Publication Data

Miller, Calvin Craig, 1954-
 Backlash : race riots in the Jim Crow Era / by Calvin Craig Miller. -- 1st
ed.
    p. cm. -- (Civil rights movement)
 Includes bibliographical references and index.
 ISBN 978-1-59935-183-4 (alk. paper)
 1. Riots--United States--History--20th century. 2. African
Americans--Crimes against--History--20th century. 3. United
States--Race
relations--History--20th century. I. Title.
 E185.61.M625 2012
 305.800973--dc22

                                        2011005673

PRINTED IN THE UNITED STATES OF AMERICA
First Edition

Book cover and interior designed by:
Ed Morgan, navyblue design studio
Greensboro, NC

Table of Contents

The exterior view of a house vandalized during the
race riots of July and August 1919 in Chicago, Illinois

1

A HISTORY
OF VIOLENCE

Studying the history of American racial violence is like watching a recurring nightmare. Similar scenes occur again and again, along with the same kinds of cruelty. Even more strikingly, the causes of these horrific events repeat themselves in one city after another.

This book tells the stories of seven of the worst examples of violence committed by white mobs against black communities in the last decade of the nineteenth century and early twentieth century. During the summer of 1919, for instance, mob violence broke out in twenty-six American cities. More than one hundred blacks died in these riots, and thousands were wounded and left homeless. With few exceptions, the rioting took place within black communities, and whites initiated the attacks. Blacks defended themselves, resulting in casualties on both sides. However, the injuries and deaths among blacks far outnumbered those among whites—to say nothing of the extensive physical damage to black neighborhoods and property.

Scholars and historians are still analyzing the reasons for these explosions of violence. But many believe the central link they shared was the legacy of slavery and the Civil War. When the Civil War ended in 1865, slavery was officially dead. But the damage it had done to the nation was far from over. The end of slavery did not necessarily mean freedom for most formerly enslaved people. African Americans in the South frequently became tenant farmers, giving their labor and most of their crops to former masters and landowners. This economic bondage was the barest of steps up from their lives on the plantations.

Former slaves were also caught up in the bitterness caused by the Reconstruction era. Reconstruction was the effort to repair the damage done by the war, restore stability to the Southern states, and help slaves make the transition to free citizenship. With emotions still raw from the war, Southerners often resented Reconstruction. Some of them claimed Northerners used African Americans of the South as allies in keeping down the white race. Secret terrorist societies, most notably the Ku Klux Klan, emerged in opposition. They sometimes resorted to lynching and torturing victims without the benefit of trial.

A white backlash against the former slaves led to the creation of a series of rigid laws to rob African Americans of basic rights. Between 1890 and 1910, every state of the former Confederacy passed legislation that came to be known as Jim Crow laws. Jim Crow laws were based upon the belief that whites were superior to blacks, and violence was often used to enforce these government-sanctioned laws, which kept the races apart in all aspects of everyday life—housing, restaurants, buses and trains, schools, hospitals, beaches and pools, water fountains, door entrances and exits, and even cemeteries. Jim Crow states also denied blacks the right to vote, by imposing literacy tests, poll taxes, and grandfather clauses,

A "colored" water cooler in a streetcar terminal in Oklahoma City, Oklahoma, in 1939.
Jim Crow laws segregated the races in former Confederate states.

which restricted the right to vote to people whose ancestors had voted before the Civil War.

To escape the oppression of Jim Crow, hundreds of thousands of blacks left the South and migrated to the North, in search of jobs and better opportunities. Between 1910 and 1920, more than 500,000 African Americans fled the South. However, when they moved north, drawn by offerings of work in urban factories, they had to take the lowest wages. And in cities like Detroit and Chicago rage among working-class whites was fueled by anxieties over competition with blacks for jobs and affordable housing.

Black soldiers returning from World War I also collided with Jim Crow laws. These returning soldiers wanted a different life in America, one consistent with the democratic principles for which the nation was fighting to ensure overseas. They no longer wanted to be treated as second-class citizens. Instead, they had hoped that their patriotic participation in the war would result in full citizenship, progress toward ending segregation, and protection from racial violence. But many whites considered the soldiers "uppity," and in no way did they want to indulge the soldiers' aspirations for equal rights. The *Shreveport Times* in Louisiana editorialized, "If the black man will stay where he belongs, act like a Negro should act, talk like a Negro should talk, and study like a Negro should study, there will be very few riots, fights, or clashes."

An African American division marching in France during WWI. African American soldiers expected to find the same freedoms they fought for overseas in place in America once they returned home.

Sadly, there were riots, and much of this violence was directed at people who had begun building more prosperous lives despite the odds against them. From Tulsa, Oklahoma, to Chicago, black businesspeople and entrepreneurs were just beginning to attain what is often called the "American Dream"—land ownership and economic stability—when attacks from white mobs ripped through their lives. Some of the bloodshed was brought on as much by envy as racial prejudice.

In East St. Louis, factory bosses tried to crush the unions by pitting black and white workers against one another. Jobs in Detroit were plentiful during World War II, but housing for the workers producing warplanes was not. The walls of segregation prevented the city from finding solutions, as white workers refused to let black families move into neighborhoods near them.

While lynching began in the rural areas, where a back road or a field at night could provide an out-of-the-way place for violence, assaults by mobs happened in the cities, where dense populations provided an abundance of potential rioters and victims. Much of the violence happened during the hot summer months, and accusations and rumor played a critical role in causing many of the riots. In Tulsa, Oklahoma, for example, a white mob of more than 10,000 attacked Tulsa's black neighborhoods after a rumor sent whites and blacks to a local courthouse—whites to defend the honor of a white girl rumored to have suffered an attempted rape by a black youth, and blacks to protect the accused youth from a rumored lynching.

Police forces of the time bear a share of the blame as well. To be sure, it is not an easy thing for police officers to always act calmly or even responsibly in the face of an advancing mob. Too often though, the police shared the racism of the perpetrators. The most indifferent officers would stand idly by as murders and burnings happened. The most violent of them would join in racial attacks. Afterwards, honest officers who had tried to do their jobs would share the stigma of those who had not.

Two of the most commonly blamed villains in modern times are politicians and the media. In the case of the race riots, office seekers and reporters often lived down to the stereotype. In Wilmington, North Carolina, and Atlanta, race-baiting politicians went on to long and successful careers, everywhere from the state house to the halls of the U.S. Congress. It is a sad truth that the worst of methods often produce reliable results in elections.

In the era of the early race riots, media meant newspapers. The newspapers often stoked race war because it drove demand for their copies sky high. Their editors and publishers were often racists, like Hoke Smith of the *Atlanta Journal* or Richard Lloyd Jones of the *Tulsa Tribune*. These publications did not hesitate to run with the wildest rumors and exaggerations of African American violence, particularly when it involved black men and white women, one of the most often repeated themes of race baiting.

Gradually, black newspapers began to provide a counterbalance as their power grew in the African American community. Alex Manly, editor of the African American *Daily Record* in Wilmington, North Carolina, was run out of town in 1898. But by the time of the Chicago riot in 1919, the city's *Defender* reported every street battle from the viewpoint of African Americans. The *Defender* even became a national publication, with circulation stretching all the way to the Deep South. The black papers could not prevent bloodshed, but they could at least see that the record was passed onto succeeding generations.

Thirteen former slaves pooled their meager resources and started the *Richmond Planet*
in Virginia. The *Planet* played an important role in molding the opinions of African
Americans across the nation. John Mitchell Jr. was not a founder of the *Richmond Planet*,
nor was he its first editor, but it was under his tenure that the *Planet* gained its well-
deserved reputation as a proponent of racial equality and rights for the African American
community. Above is a photo of the paper's composing room taken around 1898.

A Timeline of Mob Violence
in the era of Jim Crow

1898:   **Wilmington, North Carolina.** Thirty blacks were killed; the white mob suffered no casualties.

1898:   Lake City, North Carolina

1898:   Greenwood County, South Carolina

1900:   New Orleans, Louisiana

1900:   New York City, New York

1906:   **Atlanta, Georgia.** Ten blacks and two whites died; hundreds were injured.

1906:   Brownsville, Texas

1908:   **Springfield, Illinois.** Four whites and two blacks died during the three-day riot, and two blacks were lynched.

1910:   Nationwide riots—in more than twenty-five states and fifty cities—following the heavyweight championship fight between African American Jack Johnson and Jim Jeffries in Reno, Nevada, on July 4

1917:   **East St. Louis, Illinois.** Official figures say nine whites and thirty-nine blacks were killed, but the NAACP estimates that between one hundred to two hundred blacks died.

1917:   Chester, Pennsylvania

1917:   Philadelphia, Pennsylvania

1917:   Houston, Texas, Red Summer of 1919

      May 10 - Charleston, South Carolina

      May 10 – Sylvester, Georgia

      May 29 - Putnam County, Georgia

      May 31 – Monticello, Mississippi

      June 13 – New London, Connecticut

      June 13 – Memphis, Tennessee

      June 27 – Annapolis, Maryland

      June 27 – Macon, Mississippi

      July 3 – Brisbee, Arizona

      July 5 – Scranton, Pennsylvania

      July 6 – Dublin, Georgia

July 7 - Philadelphia, Pennsylvania
July 8 - Coatsville, Pennsylvania
July 9 – Tuscaloosa, Alabama
July 10 - Longview, Texas
July 11 – Baltimore, Maryland
July 15 – Port Arthur, Texas
July 19 - Washington, DC
July 21 – Norfolk, Virginia
July 23 – New Orleans, Louisiana
July 23 – Darby, Pennsylvania
July 26 – Hobson City, Alabama
July 27 - **Chicago, Illinois.** Fifteen whites and twenty-three blacks were killed; and 178 whites and 342 blacks were injured.
July 28 – Newberry, South Carolina
July 31 – Bloomington, Illinois
July 31 – Syracuse, New York
July 31 – Philadelphia, Pennsylvania
August 4 – Hattiesburg, Mississippi
August 6 – Texarkana, Texas
August 21 – New York City, New York
August 29 – Ocmulgee, Georgia
August 30 – Knoxville, Tennessee
September 28 – Omaha, Nebraska
October 1 - Elaine, Arkansas

1921: **Tulsa, Oklahoma.** Fifty whites and between 150 and two hundred blacks were killed; fire destroyed $1.5 million worth of property.

1923: Rosewood, Florida

1935: Harlem, New York

1943: **Detroit, Michigan.** Twenty-five blacks and nine whites were killed; property damage exceeded $2 million.

1943: Beaumont, Texas

1943: Harlem, New York

1943: Los Angeles, California

The light of public examination provided the cities a tool that rural areas lacked. Rural lynchers did not have to face punishment. They were able to commit their acts in secrecy and to bury the evidence. The cities did not have that convenience. The violence there had been done publicly, in the face of great outcry from black and some white media. Their determination to preserve the historical record is what eventually pushed all of the major riot cities to an attempt at reconciliation, even though it most often took decades.

An 1872 wood engraving of white men beating an African American man

2

WILMINGTON, 1898:
A DEMOCRACY
OVERTHROWN

"Send relief as soon as possible or we perish."
An unidentified African American woman

Wilmington, North Carolina, has a secret history once known only to relatively few of its own citizens. It was here that a group of conspirators used mob tactics to overthrow an elected government in 1898, the only time such an event has occurred in American history.

The violence brought a terrible end to a brilliant but short era for the state's formerly enslaved African American population. In the years between the end of the Civil War and the dawn of the twentieth century, black citizens prospered in the port city—then the state's largest city—as they did nowhere else in the state. They owned stores and homes, bought land, and ran for office.

One of the groups that helped African Americans in Wilmington succeed was the black residents who had been freed before the Civil War. John Dancy, customs collector at the time of the 1898 riot, was one of the wealthier men in the city. He was born in 1857, the son of parents set free by a slave owner. Newspaper editor Alexander Manly, born in 1866, was the son of former white governor Charles Manly. Manly had been born free. He became a skillful editor and passionate writer who fiercely defended African Americans from racist attacks. People like Dancy and Manly, who had not endured slavery, helped raise the aspirations of former slaves.

Others had taken advantage of the new freedoms formerly enslaved people gained after the Civil War. After the war ended in 1865, Congress passed legislation that put in place a policy called Reconstruction. Reconstruction was intended to restore economic and social order to the South and to insure that former slaves were not denied their citizenship rights. It was controversial among Southerners who were prone to see it as Northern vengeance against the Confederacy. Reconstruction had its successes and failures, but one of the most effective measures it instituted was the Freedmen's Bureau.

The Freedmen's Bureau helped former slaves in their transition to freedom. It handed out rations to the starving, saw to it that white bosses paid wages to black workers, and built schools, including some of the first black colleges. When slaves fled nearby war-torn plantations, they found a strong branch of the Freedmen's Bureau in Wilmington. The aid they got there helped them put down roots. African Americans became the majority in Wilmington. By 1867, 58 percent of surrounding New Hanover County was black. Many recently freed people were quick to use their newfound ability to vote. Their influence helped put African Americans on the Wilmington board of alderman and in other prominent city offices.

The presence of a black establishment in North Carolina's largest city came as a threat to many of those who had held positions of wealth and privilege in the Old South. It was also ominous to those who had most loyally served the Confederate army. They made their political alliances accordingly.

Neither political party of modern times is exactly what it was in the late nineteenth and early twentieth centuries. The Republican Party was formed in 1854 primarily in opposition to the expansion of slavery into the newly emerging western states. In the 1860 election Republican Abraham Lincoln was elected president. African Americans credited Lincoln's party for their freedom, and for the most part remained loyal to it. The Democratic Party in the South was primarily favored by the white citizens.

Abraham Lincoln in 1860

Republicans increased their power by creating political alliances, such as the one they made with the short-lived Populist Party. Disgruntled farmers originally gave the Populist Party its strength at the polls. Farmers throughout America began to feel that government served big business more faithfully than it did those who worked the land. They formed the party to speak for their interests. State legislator Daniel L. Russell helped organize the movement in North Carolina. Populists shared some goals in common with Republicans. Russell thought the Democrats too often used race as a wedge. He sought a government that would focus on what he considered more important issues, such as education and agriculture.

The Populists mounted a slow but steady march toward political power. In 1892, they elected only fourteen members to the state legislature. As expected, the Democratic legislature failed to address their concerns. In 1896, the Populists saw the time as ripe for overturning the Democrats. They joined Republicans to create a "fusion" movement.

The strategy worked. Russell was elected governor, and Populists and Republicans together gained a majority of seats in the legislature. Those who had worked together became known as Fusionists.

When the Southern Democrats lost back-to-back elections in 1894 and 1896, they became desperate and began plotting to regain power by any means possible. They settled on a message of white supremacy and the threat black men supposedly posed to white women.

It was a time ripe for demagogues and there were more than a few men eager to fill the role. Furnifold Simmons led the Democratic Party's attack on Republicans, Fusionists, and Populists for the 1898 elections.

Simmons had won election to the United States House of Representatives in 1886, but lost his seat two years later to a former slave. He was a skilled campaigner and an ardent white supremacist. He leveled numerous charges against the

Senator Furnifold Simmons in 1920

Republicans of Wilmington, accusing them of being corrupt and incompetent. But most of all, he chose to attack them not for their policies but for the race of some of their office holders.

Simmons later boasted of being the architect of a race-baiting strategy. "While we dealt with graft and advocated the free coinage of silver, the keynote of the campaign was White Supremacy, and I believe I was chiefly responsible for the choice of the issue," he said. But other prominent North Carolinians joined in hinging the election on race, including federal attorney and future governor Charles Aycock, who also gave speeches advocating white supremacy during the election.

Race-baiting was successful because it appealed to strong emotions on each side, and caused even otherwise reasonable people to fall sway to fear and anger. Rebecca Felton was a Georgia feminist, a fierce advocate for women's rights, and the first woman to serve in the U.S. Senate. She was also a racist. She made an infamous speech in 1897, saying the greatest danger farm women faced was rape by black men. She offered a dangerous solution to the problem—lynching.

"If it takes lynching to protect women's dearest possession from drunken, ravening beasts," Felton said, "then I say lynch a thousand a week."

Felton's words naturally horrified black leaders when a Wilmington newspaper published them. Alexander Manly, editor of the African American *Daily Record*, fired a broadside at Felton, along with the editors and other civic leaders who supported her. He dared to say that white and black people were equal in their sexual conduct.

Manly wrote "our experience teaches us that the women of that (white) race are not any more particular in the matter of clandestine meetings with colored men than are the white men with colored women." By changing the subject slightly, from rape to "clandestine meetings," Manly had crossed another line with the most racist of Southern whites. In their eyes, it was inconceivable that white women would have relations with black men.

With the elections of 1898 drawing near, the white supremacists prepared to seize power. They drew strength from the controversy caused by the sexual fears of the Felton-Manly exchange. The supremacists used the "Red Shirts" as their street fighting arm. Red Shirts indeed wore red shirts as a uniform at least part of the time. Different reasons are cited for the garb, from the claim they were intended to mock Northern veterans waving their "bloody shirts" from the war, to the notion that they simply wanted to stand out to those they would intimidate.

Alfred Moore Waddell became one of the leaders of the Red Shirts and one of the most eloquent orators of white supremacy. Oddly enough, he had not supported the South's secession from the Union, the event that caused the Civil War. Once the Southern states did pull out, however, he dutifully served in the Confederate Army and rose to the rank of lieutenant colonel. He was elected as a Democrat to the U.S. Congress in

1870, and served eight years. He was one of the most admired members from the South and helped investigate lawbreaking by the Ku Klux Klan.

But his actions during the 1898 election and the riot that followed showed Waddell's prejudices as not that different from Klan members. He earned the dubious honor of making one of the violent quotes of the 1898 campaign, when he threatened to "choke the current of the Cape Fear River" with black bodies. He freely admitted his part in the 1898 coup, calling it "perhaps the bloodiest race riot in North Carolina history," but he apparently felt no remorse.

The Democrats handily won the election, but widespread accounts of Red Shirt intimidation at the polls and stuffed ballot boxes poisoned the political atmosphere in Wilmington. In one case, a group of men from outside a Republican district

A group of Red Shirts poses at the polls in Scotland County, North Carolina.

showed up as workers were counting ballots. They created a distraction and even put the lights out in the polling place during the count. Some Democrats later admitted to stuffing ballot boxes with hundreds of false votes.

But Waddell and his allies knew it would take more than the election to seal their power. They planned to take bolder measures.

Some newspapers published in the evening in those days, and an advertisement appeared on the afternoon of Election Day. The announcement carried the headline "Attention White Men" and called for a whites-only meeting the next day.

A horde of white men appeared at the New Hanover County courthouse on the morning of November 9. Company laborers and their bosses showed up, as well as white tradespeople, business owners, masons, and so on. The conspirators had prepared a document in advance, so much of their business was done before the first person arrived. But the powerful men behind the scenes needed a mob to carry out the dirty work that would be needed to topple the city government. The leaders of the group called for Waddell to lead the mob, and he was delighted to take on the role.

The document they presented was bluntly racist and went straight to the point. With their "White Declaration of Independence," the writers had tried to strike a tone they considered similar to that used in the American Declaration of Independence. But the Wilmington declaration claimed a flaw in the original document of 1776. The nation's founders "did not anticipate the enfranchisement of an ignorant population of African origin." Therefore, they took upon themselves the right to ignore elections whereby such people as the Fusionists could "by means of their votes . . . dominate the intelligent and thrifty element" in the white community.

They added amendments to the "White Declaration" to enforce specific provisions of white rule in Wilmington.

Some in the crowd wanted to immediately throw out all members of the city government, but that idea was rejected. The group settled on getting rid of Mayor Silas P. Wright and Chief of Police John R. Melton. A target that aroused particular fury was newspaper editor Alexander Manly.

Again, the writers of the declaration made no secret of the violence they were willing to mete out. They seized on the editorial Manly had published in response to Rebecca Felton's call for more lynchings as evidence that he should indeed face the "justice" of the mob. Manly's article was, according to the writers, "so vile and slanderous that it would in most communities have resulted in the lynching of the editor." They called for Manly to be banished, his newspaper shut down, and his presses shipped out of the city. In fact, Manly had already fled, and his paper was no longer being published.

Alexander Manly in 1895

Yet the aroused mob still sought an outlet for its rage. The white leaders of the courthouse meeting sought to deliver an ultimatum to their black counterparts. They made a list of thirty-two prominent black men they considered to be representative leaders of the African American community. They then summoned them to the courthouse at 6 p.m. Again, Waddell was the spokesman and he made his antagonism quite clear. He told them the issue had been decided, and that there was nothing further to discuss. The sole role for the African Americans, he said, was to use their influence to help enforce the declaration, including the demand that Manly be run out of town. When one of the black representatives pointed out that they had no control over the editor, Waddell brusquely adjourned the meeting. He ordered them to send their reply to his home by 7:30 the next morning.

The African American group went to a local barber shop to discuss what to do. They faced a painful and frightening dilemma. They had not asked to be named delegates for their race in Wilmington, but had instead been selected by the worst enemies of the black community. They were also being asked to represent a white supremacist doctrine that would undo their neighbors' progress. Finally, they had been called to account for Manly's article, although the opinions were the editor's alone.

Even so, they made their best effort to write a response. They made it clear they did not speak for the editor and were in "no way responsible for, nor in any way condone, the obnoxious article that called forth your actions." But they would "most willingly use our influence to have your wishes carried out." It is questionable how "willingly" anyone could have acted under the threat of mob violence, but the drafted delegates for the black community may have thought they still stood a chance of avoiding a race war.

They picked an attorney named Armond Scott to take the message to Waddell's house. At the last minute, though, Scott found out he was on a list of people the conspirators had pledged to run out of town or worse. He decided to take the letter to the post office rather than show up at his enemy's house in person.

The next morning, Waddell waited half an hour past the appointed time before leaving home. Some people later said he knew of the letter's existence, and what it said, by the time of the deadline. If so, he chose to ignore it. He set out for the

Wilmington Light Infantry Armory, where the courthouse crowd had been told to gather with their weapons. There he met a restless crowd of about five hundred men armed with Winchester rifles and pistols. He told them that their demands had gone unanswered. His news set off a rage in the trigger-happy crowd. They now wanted vengeance, and Waddell was only too glad to lead them. He organized columns of men to march in military-style fashion through the town.

Shops and schools closed down as the mob poured into the streets. The armed men first sought to settle the score with the newspaper editor. They marched to the building which had housed Manly's office. Of course, the office had been shut down since Manly was long gone and his paper defunct, but the mob was now ruled more by anger than logic. A group of men broke inside and ransacked the place. After they smashed everything they could find inside, they doused the floors and walls with kerosene and set it on fire. Soon, the second story of the building was reduced to smoldering ash.

White supremacists destroying the *Daily Record* in Wilmington, said to be the only black-owned daily newspaper in the United States at the time

Waddell marched the men back to the armory and attempted to disperse them. "Now you have performed the duty which you have called on me to lead you to perform," he said. "Now let us go quietly to our homes and about our business and obey the law, unless we are forced in self-defense to do otherwise."

But once set loose, the vigilantes' anger was not so easily tamed. They at first set up patrols of every block in the city, four men to a block, but with tensions running so high, it was not long before all order gave way. What may have looked like an army when Waddell was leading it soon broke into separate mobs seeking bloodshed wherever they could find or make it.

They raged through the city throughout the day, sparking gunfights in black business districts and homes. The first cross-fire between black and white gunmen broke out at the intersection of Fourth and Harnett streets. The battle also produced the first casualties, when bullets struck one white man and six black men, with two of them killed instantly. The white mob fanned out into the African American neighborhood of Brooklyn, terrorizing residents and firing into houses. It was not long before they started setting homes on fire.

A black politician named Daniel Wright became a target when rumors spread that he had shot the white man at Fourth and Harnett. Red Shirts surrounded his house and fired into it. Wright fired back, killing two of his attackers. The Red Shirts at last pulled him from his house, and someone bloodied his head with a pipe. Another of his attackers suggested Wright be allowed a short head start to run for it, a false mercy since he had barely started running when gunmen began pouring bullets into him. He lay in the street for more than an hour before anyone took him to the hospital. He died the next day. Forty rounds were lodged in his body.

Confusion reigned as newspapers attempted to publish accounts of what was happening. With gunfire exploding in

A Red Shirt rally in front of James Sanitarium in Laurinburg, North Carolina, in 1898

the streets outside their offices, reporting the news was no easy task. Accurate accounts of the number of people killed and wounded varied widely at the time, as they do to this day. Reports put the number as low as nine and as high as the hundreds. Violence was abundant and random. Some of the rioters caught the trolleys home and fired their weapons into houses as they passed black neighborhoods, not knowing or caring whom they hit.

Not all of the white people shared the bloodlust of the vigilantes and Red Shirts. James Sprunt, the white owner of a cotton warehouse called the Sprunt Cotton Compress, employed many black workers. When news of the violence reached the warehouse, Sprunt invited workers and their wives to stay inside for protection.

A crowd of white gunmen surrounded the place when they heard a black "mob" had assembled there. The white attackers attempted to recruit military men to lead them, but without much success. When they appointed Colonel Roger Moore as their leader, he told them he would have anyone who fired into the warehouse arrested. They turned to Captain Donald MacRae, a Spanish-American War veteran, in another attempt to find a leader. He too cautioned against violence. He later recalled that "as few of the negroes were armed, it was little less than murder that they [the crowd of whites] proposed." The incident at the warehouse ended in a standoff.

Entire families retreated into the woods around the city, frightened or burned out of their homes. For days, they huddled in the cold near the Cape Fear River, trying to scrounge for food and evade their attackers. Before it was over, most had fled the city forever.

Three days after the riots, an African American woman wrote President William McKinley, "[T]oday, we are mourners in a strange land with no protection near. God help us." The woman's name does not appear in the letter, because she said she could not sign her name and live. In another letter to McKinley, the author wrote, "[A]re we to die like rats in a trap?"

Even before the riots ended, Waddell set about the business of reaping the rewards. He and the other conspirators got everything they had demanded in the New Hanover County Courthouse. They forced the mayor and police chief to resign, along with the entire board of aldermen. The Democrats and the conspirators replaced elected officials with men of their own choosing. Waddell announced that he would return peace and order to the city, but the aftermath seemed little different than the mob atmosphere of the riot. The leaders of the riots, including military veterans, marched Republicans out of town at bayonet point while crowds jeered and packed them on trains leading out of the city. The overthrow of the government was now complete.

Wilmington paid a dear price to the ambitions of Waddell, the Red Shirts, and the conspirators. It lost an entire class of successful entrepreneurs and business people who might have continued to build the city.

The conspirators painted their revolution as a victory for white people, but it was no such thing. Even during Reconstruction, African Americans had continued to work for lower wages, a consequence of centuries of African American slavery. As they had promised, the Democrats fired black city workers and gave their jobs to whites—but they kept all city salaries at the low level of "black wages."

The organizers of the bloodiest days in Wilmington's history never faced any kind of justice. Quite the contrary, they achieved political success.

Alfred Moore Waddell took over as mayor, serving until 1905. In 1899, former U.S. attorney Charles Aycock worked with state legislators to take the vote away from black people, with gimmicks such as poll taxes and the "grandfather clause," stipulating that one could vote if one's grandfather had voted, which naturally ruled out former slaves. Aycock was elected governor in 1901 on a white supremacy platform. Furnifold Simmons was elected to the United States Senate in 1900 and served for thirty years. Their personal success, achieved by bloodshed, came at the expense of people who had worked for what they had, as well as anyone else who had ever sought racial and class justice in North Carolina.

A view of downtown Wilmington around 1900

1898 Monument and Memorial Park

In November 2008, more than a century after the riots, the city of Wilmington, North Carolina, dedicated a monument and memorial park to commemorate the lives lost in 1898. Just blocks from where the first shots were fired, at the northern gateway to the city, are six, cast-bronze paddles, each standing sixteen-feet high and weighing one thousand pounds. The paddles symbolize the presence of water. "In many African traditions, water is believed to be a medium for the transition between the worlds of the living and the dead," the sculptor Ayokunle Odeleye said. "The use of paddle imagery memorializes not only the destruction of the community, but the collective coexistence of the two races at a unique time in history." Funding for the memorial came entirely from Wilmington businesses and residents, including descendants of the men who planned the bloody coup.

3

Atlanta, 1906: Politics in a Powder Keg

"In the flickering light the mob swayed, paused, and began to flow toward us. In that instant . . . I knew then who I was. I was a Negro . . . which marked me a person to be hunted, hanged, discriminated against, kept in poverty and ignorance, in order that those whose skin was white would have readily at hand a proof of their superiority."

Thirteen-year-old Walter White

Atlanta entered the early years of the twentieth century as the flagship city of the "New South," a progressive metropolis seeking to move beyond the legacy of slavery. Building and construction boomed, and jobs were plentiful. African Americans prospered along with their white neighbors, despite having to deal with segregation and prejudice. Atlanta boasted six black colleges and some of the greatest African American intellectuals, including W. E. B. Du Bois, one of the founders of the National Association for the Advancement of Colored People (NAACP). The city's leaders proudly noted that Atlanta had never had a race riot.

Atlanta offered opportunities for the ambitious. It was a fitting home for two strong-willed men who competed for the governor's seat in 1906. The contest was a battle between two rival newspaper publishers. Both Clark Howell and Hoke Smith had come from well-educated, respected families. Howell owned the *Atlanta Constitution*, while Smith published the rival *Atlanta Journal*.

Clark Howell was born on September 21, 1863. His father Evan was an artillery officer in the Civil War. After the war, Evan became a reporter for the *Atlanta Intelligencer*. In 1876, Evan Howell bought partial ownership of the *Constitution*. Clark Howell graduated from the University of Georgia at

Athens in 1883, then traveled north to work on big city newspapers, including the *New York Times*. In 1884, he moved back to Atlanta and took a job as a night editor at his father's paper. He combined his two passions, journalism and politics, writing strongly opinionated pieces for the paper and running for office. In 1885, he ran a successful campaign for election to the Georgia House of Representatives, and was twice reelected.

Clark Howell in 1914

Howell steadily climbed the ladder in both his careers. In 1900, he was elected to the state Senate. The following year, he bought enough stock in the *Atlanta Constitution* to take over control of the paper. Owning a newspaper and winning elections set Howell on an ambitious political path, and in 1906, he entered the race for governor. The chief obstacle in his path was Hoke Smith.

Hoke Smith

Education helped put bread on the table during Hoke Smith's childhood. He was born on September 2, 1855, in Newton, North Carolina. His father Hildreth was the president of Catawba College, his mother Mary a daughter of a well-to-do Southern family. His family moved to Chapel Hill in 1857, when his father took a faculty position at the University of North Carolina. Hildreth took charge of his son's education while the Civil War raged. Three years after the war ended, Hildreth lost his job with the university. The family moved to Atlanta where Hildreth took a job in the city's public schools.

In his new hometown Smith read for a career as a lawyer at an Atlanta law firm, passing the bar exam when he was only seventeen. He took on personal injury cases, frequently fighting the powerful railroads on behalf of working-class clients. Since his family was able to offer him little financial support, he became quite frugal with money, even sleeping in his office when funds were short. Gradually, he accumulated wealth and became a prominent member of Atlanta society. Smith ran successfully for the city school board and rose to the position of board president. In 1887, he spent $10,000 to buy the *Atlanta Journal*. In a little more than a decade, he gained back his investment many times over. His paper became the main rival of the *Atlanta Constitution*.

Both Smith and Howell tried to cast the other as "soft" on the issue of race. In fact, both ran racist campaigns. Both wanted to keep African American voters from the ballot boxes. Although the city had a reputation of openness, Atlanta had already done quite a bit to suppress black voters, including setting a poll tax that many people barely more than a generation out of slavery could not afford to pay. Smith wanted to disenfranchise African Americans—to strip them of their voting rights. Howell was just as much of a white supremacist, but he thought that previous measures had done enough to make sure their numbers at the polls remained low. Black Atlantans found themselves with no friends in the governor's race.

Each of the candidates published newspapers, giving them greater circulation for their racist views. Throughout the summer, both Howell's *Constitution* and Smith's *Journal* churned out stories about black misconduct and crime, particularly rape. The editors of *Atlanta News* and the *Atlanta Georgian*, both stridently anti black publications, enthusiastically joined the smear.

Editors wrote rants about the supposed dangers caused by black men who hung out in bars, drinking liquor from bottles illustrated with explicit pictures of white women, and being turned into creatures of lust. The stories brought out the worst in many of their readers.

THE TWO PLATFORMS

Every RADICAL in Congress VOTED for NEGRO SUFFRAGE.   Every RADICAL in the Pennsylvania Senate VOTED for NEGRO SUFFRAGE.
STEVENS, FORNEY & CAMERON are for NEGRO SUFFRAGE; they are all Candidates for the UNITED STATES SENATE.   NO RADICAL NEWSPAPER OPPOSES NEGRO SUFFRAGE.
GEARY said in a Speech, at Harrisburg, 11th of August, 1866—"THERE CAN BE NO POSSIBLE OBJECTION TO NEGRO SUFFRAGE."

CLYMER'S
Platform is for the White Man.

GEARY'S
Platform is for the Negro.

READ THE PLATFORMS

CONGRESS says, THE NEGRO MUST BE ALLOWED TO VOTE, OR THE STATES BE PUNISHED.

[POST THIS UP.]

A racist campaign poster from 1866 depicting the division between the "radical" Republicans and the Democrats. Such attitudes continued through many elections, threatening the black vote.

The *Journal* urged men to arm their wives and daughters with guns, and teach them how to shoot, supposedly to defend themselves against would-be black assailants. As fears of a full-blown race war spread, gun merchants did a booming business.

The newspapers attacked the black "dives," bars frequented by black men. White editors stirred up fears that the patrons, staring at pictures of scantily clad white women that were rumored to hang in the bars, would become violent and attack real women. Lewd rumors about such places were easy to spread among the readership because the majority of white people never went into black bars.

People who drank in bars were not the only targets of white suspicion and violence. A theater was staging Thomas Dixon's play *The Clansman*, a story glorifying the Ku Klux Klan, adding its message of race hatred to the already dangerous brew of racial fear and suspicion. When a black train porter grasped a white woman's arm to help her on board, he caught the attention of a group of people on horses on their way to the theater. They seized him, whipped him, and drove him out of town.

The papers mixed stories of assault, chance insults, and real crimes to make it seem as if black men were roaming the streets almost every hour of the day seeking white women. Rape was the greatest of all fears, and the papers ruthlessly exploited it. Black males began to avoid any contact with white women, since it took very little to become a suspected rapist.

One woman described her surprise at the fear a black man showed at an accidental touch. A young man in a hurry came out of a doorway onto the sidewalk, and brushed against her, arm against arm. "When he turned and found it was a white woman he had touched, such a look of abject terror and fear came into his face as I hope never again to see on a human countenance," she told an interviewer. "He knew what it meant if I was frightened, called for help, and accused him of insulting or attacking me." The young man ran for his life and ducked into an alley.

In incidents like this, African American fears of being falsely accused, particularly in the media, were quite justified.

This was in the day of the "extra," special newspaper editions put out when news was happening quickly. The papers published extras almost every time a story hinged on race. The newspapers seemed determined to set off a race war, and in late September, they succeeded.

On the morning of September 22, a black man was reported to have approached the home of Mary Chafin, who lived just outside Atlanta. He first asked her if a John Brown lived there. On being told no, he then asked for a drink of water, and Chafin directed him to a nearby spring. Several hours later she reported finding him in her barn, and chased him away with a shotgun.

This was just the kind of narrative the papers were the quickest to report. The afternoon headline in the *Journal* read "NEGRO ATTEMPTS TO ASSAULT MRS. MARY CHAFIN NEAR SUGAR CREEK BRIDGE."

A second minor incident followed, with equally dramatic and deliberately frightening coverage. A woman identified in news accounts as Mrs. Frank Arnold was reportedly grabbed by the arm by a black man, who said "Come on, honey, and go with me." She screamed, a family member came, and he ran away. The *Evening News* trumpeted "SECOND ASSAULT."

A little later, a teenager named Alma Allen reported that she had been grabbed from behind by a black man who threw her against her house and ran away. The extra edition quickly hit the streets. "THIRD ASSAULT" the headline shouted.

Several thousand people, mostly men and boys, who had been drinking in nearby taverns, spilled onto Peachtree, Decatur, Pryor, Whitehall, Broad, and other downtown streets.

City officials tried to calm the angry crowds. Mayor James G. Woodward and other city officials made speeches in the street, warning would-be rioters that any mass violence would only scar the reputation of Atlanta. But the crowd's anger and

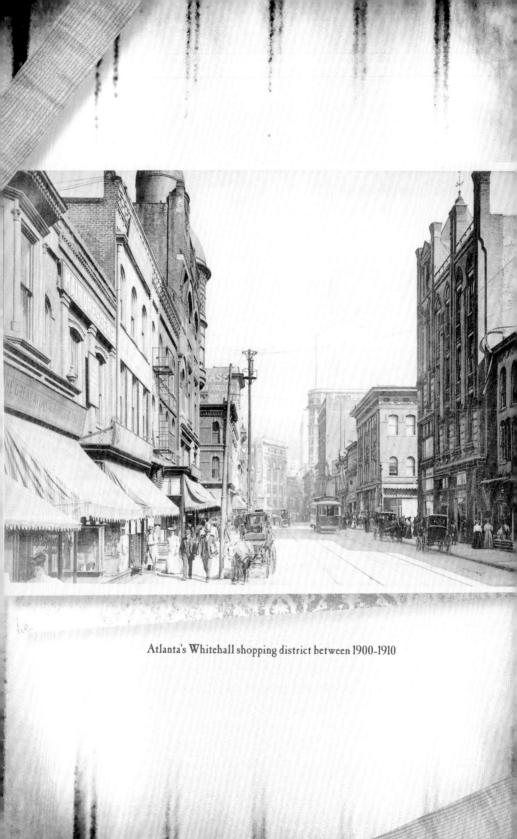

Atlanta's Whitehall shopping district between 1900-1910

fear now ruled them, and they were in no mood to listen to reason. They shouted down the speakers, jeering and yelling racial slurs.

Rumors of a fourth assault fueled their rage beyond any hope of reason. Rioting began to break out shortly before businesses closed for the night. At that time, businesses closed down at ten in the evening. As the saloons closed down, a Saturday night crowd of drinkers swelled the ranks of the rioters.

They tore through the downtown business district, attacking people and black businesses. Any African American became fair game. White men broke into a barbershop owned by Alonzo Herndon, a former slave turned entrepreneur. They murdered the barbers, stole their clothes as souvenirs, and dumped the bodies in an alley. Others boarded streetcars, let the white passengers get off, and savagely attacked African American riders.

Some public officials tried to stop the violence, while others egged it on. A few policemen risked the wrath of the crowds to save individual black citizens. Others stood by and watched. The mayor ordered that fire hoses be turned on the mob, but even the blast of water on a winter night was not enough to stop them. The victims of the riot were sprayed as well, with one black man killed when he was knocked down by the hoses.

A boy named Walter White, age thirteen at the time, witnessed one of the first assaults at a barbershop. He watched as a young black boy handicapped by a withered foot had run out of the shop, only to be run down and clubbed to death by rampaging thugs.

White ran home only to find that the downtown mobs had spread into African American neighborhoods. His father was a mail carrier of mixed racial heritage, with skin so white that he was able to "pass" as white, as the rest of the family did.

People in the neighborhood knew the family was of mixed descent and that was enough to make them a target.

The mob surged onto the street where the Whites lived and moved closer to their yard. People who had coexisted peacefully with the Whites for years screamed threats and racial slurs at them. The son of a grocer with whom they did business yelled for the crowd to burn down the Whites' house. The father and his son guarded their windows with rifles.

Years later, White still remembered his father's command. "Son, don't shoot until the first man puts his foot on the lawn and then—don't you miss!" the elder White said. White would go on to become head of the NAACP and a crusading investigator of racial violence.

The boy did not have to fire. Shots rang out from a two-story building nearby, and the mob stopped. The show of resistance was enough to send them in search of easier targets.

Finally, aided by a heavy rain that helped disperse the mobs, the state militia managed to gain control of the city early Sunday morning, although racial flare-ups continued for several days.

On Monday, a group of African American men gathered at nearby Brownsville, a small town which had two black colleges, Clark College and Gammon Theological Seminary. They wanted to fight fire with fire and had armed themselves with rifles and guns. When the police found out, they attacked the gathering. The shootout left one police officer dead.

The attendees of the twentieth annual session of the NAACP in Cleveland, Ohio, in 1929. Founded in 1909, the organization's mission is "to ensure the political, educational, social, and economic equality of rights of all persons and to eliminate racial hatred and racial discrimination."

The state militia then arrested more than 250 African American men.

No one is sure how many people died in the rioting. The city coroner only issued ten death certificates, but that number is suspiciously low. Other estimates place the body count at twenty-five to forty African Americans. Most sources place the number of white deaths at two, with one of them a woman whose heart attack was likely triggered by fear of the mobs.

After the riot, Atlanta leaders tried to heal the scars from the bloodshed. The event did tremendous damage to the city reputation, both in the United States and internationally. Newspapers in Europe covered the riot extensively, in part because its excesses appeared similar to those against the continent's Jews, then an oppressed minority. Most of the American national press rebuked Atlanta's leaders for allowing such a bloodbath.

The city responded by setting up commissions of inquiry and civic groups to seek solutions. But it remained unclear that Atlanta's ruling elite had learned anything from the experience. Most of them blamed blacks for the riot. The Committee of Ten, a group of ten of the city's most prominent white men, attempted to show the nation that Atlanta could heal itself. The committee announced that both white and black rioters would receive justice in the courts. Yet the courts' justice was questionable at best. The one person to receive an extremely harsh punishment was a black man who drew a life sentence for murder. Whites were also punished, but most of them only served a month in jail.

The investigating committees did fault the newspapers for their fanning of the flames. But the Atlanta newspapers continued their one-sided reporting of news involving race, and some northern journalists even defended the riot. The *New York World* ran an article defending the violence against Atlanta's African American citizens, saying it was necessary to protect white women. Atlanta publisher J. Max Barber angrily rebutted the writer. Barber, who owned the publication *Voice of the Negro*, blamed the white Atlanta newspapers for setting up "a frightful carnival of newspaper lies." He condemned Hoke Smith for exploiting race in his campaign for governor. Chairman James W. English of the Committee of Ten summoned Barber for a meeting soon after he published these words.

If Barber hoped for reconciliation, he was disappointed. Instead, English threatened him and told him he should "straighten [himself] out with . . . white people at once." English, who was also the police commissioner, warned Barber he could end up on a chain gang if he defied English's wishes. The African American publisher instead chose to leave Atlanta for Chicago. Hundreds of Atlanta's black leaders also left the city, depriving it of many who might have contributed to its success.

The trouble with the city's investigating committees was they started from a prejudiced viewpoint. They were willing to meet with black leaders, but still believed the races should be segregated. Underneath their righteous proclamations, many of the white leaders still saw black people as did their fathers and grandfathers in the plantation days before the Civil War. They were more concerned about image than justice.

Hoke Smith won the 1906 election for governor. He immediately set out to fulfill his racist campaign promises. In 1907, he pushed a bill through the state legislature that effectively took the vote away from African Americans. The light punishment handed out to white rioters may have well contributed to a rise of the Ku Klux Klan in the teen years of the twentieth century, and a wave of lynchings that continued into the 1920s.

As did most cities that were damaged by race riots, the city eventually did confront its responsibility for the violence.

COPYRIGHT- 1923
THE HAMMOND STUDIOS,
MERIDIAN, AND JACKSON, MISS

An initiation ceremony of the Ku Klux Klan in 1923.

Today students in the city schools learn the history of the infamous events of 1906. In 2006, the city held a commemoration of the riot's hundredth anniversary. Guides offered walking tours of the areas hardest hit by the bloodshed.

W. E. B. Du Bois was one of those who left the city afterward. He expressed the feelings of many who no longer felt at home in Atlanta. In a poem, he later wrote "Is this Thy Justice, O Father, that guile be easier than innocence and the innocent be crucified for the guilt of the untouched guilty?" The failure to protect the innocent and punish the guilty was a burden Atlanta carried through the early decades of the twentieth century.

4

SPRINGFIELD, 1908: MURDER IN THE CITY OF LINCOLN

"I ain't got a thing left in the world but my panama hat."
James "Dandy Jim" Smith, a black saloonkeeper

The race riot of 1908 is a painful chapter in the history of Springfield, Illinois. The city was the hometown of Abraham Lincoln, the sixteenth president and one of the most revered statesmen in American history. Lincoln led the country through the Civil War and helped destroy the system of African American slavery. He issued the Emancipation Proclamation of 1863, which declared freedom for Southern slaves. No American president is more revered for his contributions to racial equality. Springfield was proud of its most famous son.

The 1908 race riot tarnished Springfield's legacy. One of the frightening things about the violence was the involvement of ordinary people. The people who started it and carried out its atrocities were not ambitious politicians or powerful media figures. They were average citizens, neighbors of the people they attacked, beat, and murdered.

One of the causes of racial friction was competition for jobs. The supply of jobs was not enough to match the number of job seekers. Many white people resented having to compete with blacks for menial work in factories and coal mines. Some of the African Americans had fled the South, hoping

Cotton workers in Charlotte, North Carolina, around 1900. This type of labor, similar to work done by slaves, motivated many African Americans to leave the South in hopes of finding better opportunities for advancement.

to gain some of the advantages of urban living and to leave behind the racial bigotry of a region that had so recently used black people as slaves.

But in the early 1900s, racism pervaded the entire country. Economic hardship only made it worse. And some in Springfield were quick to blame African Americans for any social problem, crime, or act of violence. Newspapers fanned the flames with exaggerated accounts of every reported or invented misdeed by a black person. With racial resentment smoldering during the long hot summer of 1908, all that was needed was a spark to set off a race war.

The spark came on the night of July 4. Clergy Ballard, a mining engineer, awoke to the sound of someone moving about in his house. He found a black man standing by the bedside of his daughter, according to what he later told police. He chased the man out of his house and followed, trying to catch him. Racing after the intruder proved to be a fatal mistake. When Ballard did catch up with the man, the burglar slashed his throat with a straight razor.

Ballard died the next morning. But before he did, he told them his story about the man hovering over his daughter's bed and identified his assailant. He said it was Joe James, a black man who had a record of petty crimes. James was arrested and locked in the downtown jail, charged with murder and attempted rape.

Another reported assault more than a month later added to the suspicion of African Americans. Mabel Hallam told police that on the night of August 13, a black man dragged her from her bed and raped her. Hallam identified the alleged rapist as George Richardson. Unlike James, Richardson had no criminal record. He was a poor laborer who had been taking temporary work from homeowners to support himself.

The *Illinois State Journal* and other newspapers acted no more responsibly in their reporting than had the Atlanta papers. On the morning following Mabel Hallam's report to the police, the bold *Journal* headline proclaimed "DRAGGED FROM HER BED AND OUTRAGED BY NEGRO." Police arrested Richardson, charged him with rape, and put him in the same jail as Joe James.

But ordinary criminal justice was not fast enough for some people in Springfield. By three in the afternoon, a mob had gathered outside the jail, with its ringleaders demanding the prisoners be turned over to them. Sheriff Charles Werner realized how dangerous the situation was becoming and devised a plan to get his two inmates to another jail. He contacted Harry Loper, a local restaurant owner, for help with a getaway plan. Sheriff Werner had a fire alarm set off as a diversion, and then rushed the two men out of the jail, down the alley, and into Loper's car. Loper drove the two inmates to the McLean County jail in Bloomington. When the mob discovered how the police had fooled them, they tore on a rampage through the city.

Loper later said he had offered to help the sheriff quell the riot because he had seen a race riot in Cincinnati, Ohio, and did not wish to see such violence in Springfield. Loper's peaceful intentions amounted to race treachery, though, in the eyes of the angry crowd. One of Loper's fellow downtown businesspeople was Kate Howard, a local innkeeper whose hatred of African Americans was well-known around town. Howard urged the mob to attack Loper's restaurant. They smashed Loper's windows, burned down his building, and set his car on fire. They wanted to lynch Loper as well, but he hid in the basement of the restaurant and managed to escape before being burned alive.

By the time the rioters had finished their revenge on Loper, about 5,000 people had gathered in Springfield's streets.

The mob surged into a small downtown black business district called the Levee, breaking shop windows and helping themselves to the merchandise. What they did not steal, they destroyed. They crashed through thirty-five businesses, kicking down doors, smashing windows, and firing bullets into buildings.

"If a cyclone had passed that way it would have done no more damage," wrote the *Springfield News*.

The worst was yet to come. One of the stores the rioters looted was a pawn shop, and from it they took guns and rope. These were the tools they would use in grisly acts of violence.

The crowd poured into the Badlands, a predominately African American neighborhood of mostly small houses. One of the mob's first targets was a barbershop owned by Scott Burton. Newspaper stories differed on the details of Burton's murder. Some said he was sitting quietly inside when the mob reached his door, while others claimed he defended his shop with a shotgun. What is certain is that the mob attacked him, dragged him into the street, and beat him savagely, with everything from bottles to an ax. They then dragged him to a tree and lynched him. The rioters had by then descended to ghoulish glee at their feat, and delighted in swinging and mutilating Burton's body. For days afterward, they hacked off pieces of the tree for souvenirs.

After Burton's murder, the mob set about the business of destroying every black-owned home they could get their hands on. White residents began hanging sheets outside their windows, a signal to show that there were only white people inside. The rioters charged into African American homes and wrecked them much as they had trashed the shops, pulled mattresses from the beds, soaked them with kerosene, and set them on fire.

By the time the fires blazed through the Badlands, a crowd of 12,000 had poured into the streets to watch or participate.

The ring of the fire bell mingled with the echoes of gunfire and the howl of dogs sent into frenzy by the human violence. When fire trucks arrived, the mob refused to let them douse the flames and even cut some of the hoses.

Black people ran for their lives. Some of their white neighbors let them in and hid them in their homes, a brave act under the circumstances. Others turned them away. Thousands of residents fled Springfield, many of them for good. When the Illinois militia arrived at the State Arsenal, some African Americans gathered there for refuge. The soldiers became their only defense against the mobs.

The militia's protection of blacks, however, made it a target of the next wave of violence Saturday evening. A crowd of hopeful lynchers and rioters gathered at the Old Courthouse Building, and marched toward the arsenal, intending to attack the black refugees sheltered there. The militia cavalry stopped the marchers in their tracks.

The mob altered its path of the previous night, when the rioters had chosen mostly poor neighborhoods for their violence. Most of the people attacked the first night were random victims who had been unlucky enough to cross paths with the mob. On Saturday night, the rioters changed tactics, and selected a victim whose assault could send a message.

William Donigan was an elderly black man who had lived in the city since his teens. At age eighty-four, he had accomplished much. He had begun his career as a shoemaker, and he had used his money to buy real estate. By the time of the riots, he was a well-to-do African American. This would have been reason enough for the mob to attack him. But Donigan had committed another infraction of the racist social order. For twenty years, he had been married to Sarah Rudolph, a white woman. For many whites, racial intermarriage aroused a special fury. They decided to make Donigan pay a bloody price for his marriage and success.

Soldiers in mess tents during the Springfield, Illinois, riots

The Donigan family was fearful from the moment they learned the mob was on the march. They telephoned the authorities and were promised soldiers would come to protect them, but none did. The mob smashed through Donigan's door at about nine that night. They grabbed the elderly man and hauled him out of his house. He cried out for mercy, but the mob slashed his throat, and hanged him from a tree so short his feet touched the ground. When the police finally arrived and cut him down they took Donigan to the hospital, where he died the next morning of his wounds.

"They say my uncle was killed because he [was] married to a white woman, but they have been married twenty years," a nephew said. "He was even told by some of the ringleaders of the mob that he had too much property for a nigger."

William Donigan was the last victim of the Springfield riots. The city's official count put the total number of dead at seven, but some people accused the city of covering up other deaths. The rioting destroyed forty homes and shut down twenty-four businesses.

The aftermath of the violence did such damage to the city's property and reputation as to shock its officials into action. Governor Charles Deneen promised that those who had broken the law in their rampage would quickly face trial. The newspapers called for a return to law and order. But again the system failed African American victims. A grand jury handed down more than one hundred indictments, but the defendants went in front of sympathetic all-white juries. Only one man received a short jail sentence.

Governor Charles Deenen

After being arrested in the lynching of Scott Burton, Kate Howard poisoned herself and died in police custody. Mabel Hallam later recanted her charge of rape against George Richardson. Richardson went free, but Joe James was hanged for the murder of Clergy Ballard. It seemed that the swift justice promised by the governor applied only to African Americans found guilty.

The shock of seeing a city outside the former Confederacy explode in racial violence caused a national outcry for justice. Although Abraham Lincoln's legacy had not stopped the race riot in his hometown, the symbolic significance of such an outrage in a city that might have claimed a more honorable place in history helped fuel a desire to make things right again. The greatest legacy of Springfield was the birth of the National Association for the Advancement of Colored People (NAACP).

The roots of the NAACP were first planted in the Niagara Movement of 1905. Black leaders met on the Canadian side of Niagara Falls with the intention of taking a stand for racial equality and against lynching and other forms of terrorism against African Americans. Prominent scholars such as W. E. B. Du Bois and William Trotter, both among the earliest black graduates of Harvard, joined to assemble the group. They convened a meeting of about sixty prominent African Americans to establish a set of organizing principles. But the movement ran into trouble raising enough money to stay afloat, and disagreements among its members snagged its agenda. By 1910, the Niagara Movement had dissolved.

The Springfield riot threw a harsh light on the injustices suffered by African Americans and helped build support for the NAACP. William English Walling and his wife Anna Strunsky, both of them wealthy advocates of social reform, traveled to Springfield to report on the riots. They had previously gone to Russia to write about conditions under the czars, tyrannical rulers who brutally repressed their citizens and persecuted the Jews. The viciousness of the Springfield riot

Niagara Movement leaders W. E. B. Du Bois (seated),
and (left to right) J. R. Clifford, L. M. Hershaw, and
F. H. M. Murray at Harpers Ferry in 1906

convinced them America's treatment of African Americans was worse. The czars had to order their persecutions, but in Springfield the violence arose from the people, neighbors of the citizens they beat, murdered, and robbed. The couple was shocked by the fact that those responsible bragged about it afterwards.

Walling's report on Springfield in the September 1908 edition of the *Independent* helped spread their shock through the circles of prominent and wealthy people. New York journalist Mary White Ovington immediately wrote a letter to Walling, telling him of her desire to help in the struggle against racial injustice. The two joined with Henry Moskovitz, a doctor of philosophy, to become the first white members of the group that would become the NAACP. They contacted Du Bois, anti-lynching activist Ida Bell Wells-Barnett, attorney and journalist Archibald Henry Grimké, and many other prominent social crusaders to lay the groundwork. The group's first statement appeared on February 12, 1909, the one-hundredth anniversary of Lincoln's birth.

The association held its first meeting in New York several months later. The NAACP became the most prominent civil rights organization of the twentieth century. It would wage a long campaign against lynching, segregation, and discrimination.

The founding of the premier civil rights organization in the country gave a measure of redemption to Springfield. It showed that even a terrible tragedy can be used for good ends by people determined to seek justice. The NAACP marked the riot as one of the central events in its history, but civil rights leaders were ever mindful of another lesson as they continued their struggle. If a race riot could happen in a place so proud of its role in the history of racial progress, no city was immune.

5

EAST ST. LOUIS, 1917: WORKER AGAINST WORKER

"What I saw before me as I stepped outside had been described at church that Sunday by the Reverend in dark, spine-chilling tones. This was the Apocalypse. Clouds, glowing from the incandescent light of huge flames leaping upward from the riverbank, raced across the sky . . . but not as quickly as the breathless figures that dashed in all directions. The entire black community appeared to be fleeing."
Eleven-year-old Freda Josephine McDonald

East St. Louis could be a hard city in the early twentieth century. Among its biggest industries were meat-packing and metal ore processing plants, both of which often had miserable working conditions and paid low wages. The city was crime ridden, with prostitutes and thieves loitering in the roughest parts of town. Slums sprang up in the shadows of the factories. The smell of soot from the ore plants lingered in the streets.

But to African Americans in the South, the city offered an escape from the racial repression of the South. Also, an infestation of boll weevils attacked the cotton crops, and an economic recession swept the region. By contrast, East St. Louis seemed a better alternative, even with the low wages and harsh working conditions.

When America entered World War I in April of 1917, the factories lost many of their young male workers to military service and jobs became more available. Labor recruiters traveled to the South seeking workers for the factories. This increased the number of black workers moving north.

A 1917 World War I poster calling for workers to help support the war effort

IF YOU CAN USE TOOLS
YOU ARE WANTED

Your country needs ships and men to build them. Armies, munitions and supplies are useless in this war without ships to transport them. Go to the nearest shipyard and offer your services. You can thus help to win the war and make the world safe for Democracy.

However, many of those who arrived in East St. Louis found themselves in the middle of a dispute between factory owners and workers. In 1916, the Aluminum Ore Employees Protective Association, a worker's union, staged a strike against the Aluminum Ore Company. They won some concessions, but in retaliation the ore company began to hire black workers and to fire white workers. From the company's point of view they were replacing white troublemakers with workers who would be more appreciative of the job. The company's policy achieved its goal of dividing workers, but at the price of sowing future violence.

The newest citizens of East St. Louis also found themselves embroiled in election year politics. In the 1916 election, President Woodrow Wilson, a Democrat, was running for reelection. However, the Democratic Party's chances did not look good in Illinois.

Democrats and Republicans preached the same party policies that had drawn the battle lines in the Wilmington, North Carolina, riot. The Republicans were considered advocates of racial justice as the "party of Lincoln," and their reputation was closely linked to the end of slavery. The Democrats usually supported the status quo in racial relations, which meant standing for the old system of racial segregation in the South and for white privilege everywhere else in America.

Democrats in Illinois viewed the migration of black workers to East St. Louis with suspicion. They began to describe the recruitment of black workers as "colonization," meaning the factory owners had attempted to make a black colony in the city to undercut the white workers. The Democrats made the word "colonization" a household term. As they feared, Illinois Democrats lost the 1916 election, although President Wilson won another term as president. But the race-baiting politicians did win a dubious victory. They made white working-class families fear the movement of African Americans into Illinois as a danger to their livelihood. Bad feelings lingered after the election.

Suspicion and fear between the races smoldered through the early months of 1917. Fights and assaults between blacks and whites flared throughout the late winter. As the spring of 1917 approached, a feeling of menace pervaded the city. White workers worried the factories would replace them altogether with African Americans, and black workers worried that another northern city would turn out to be a false haven for their dreams of freedom and security.

The labor unions thought the legions of black workers would ruin their chances to stage any strike of the predominately white work force. In May, they decided to plead their case to the city council. On the day of the meeting, an ad ran in a local newspaper, that read "Negro and cheap foreign labor [is being imported by the Aluminum Ore Company] to tear down the standard of living of our citizens. Imported gunmen, detectives, and federal injunctions are being used to crush our people. Come and hear the truth that the press will not publish."

On the evening of May 28, union members turned out in full force. Their supporters packed the auditorium for the council meeting. They cheered when a group of union women showed up in their finest dresses, hoping to impress the mayor and council members that they were examples of white women whose livelihood was threatened by the arrival of black southern workers. The crowd grew so large that seating ran out, and those sympathetic with the union gathered on the streets outside.

Mayor Fred Mollman spoke first. In an attempt to head off complaints that the city had not done enough to protect white workers' jobs, the mayor said the council was working on a plan to keep black workers from coming to the city. He pointed out that he had contacted southern governors for their assistance in persuading black people in the South that

East St. Louis did not have enough jobs to make the journey there worthwhile.

One union member after another spoke, almost all of them saying that black workers were destroying the working class, the unions, and the city. They talked of street crimes such as robberies, in which black gunmen attacked and robbed white citizens and were allowed to go free. How this could have happened without there being more notice was not made clear. Anger filled the hall.

A local lawyer tapped into the rage and intentionally tried to spark it into violence. Alexander Flannigen was familiar to many people there, since he had once been the city treasurer and sold real estate from his downtown office. He was an expert speaker who knew how to warm up a crowd with a few jokes. However, his real message was anything but a joke. Flannigen warned that blacks hurt the local housing market, claiming that houses sold to them became rundown and lowered the value of nearby homes. He then offered a rather dangerous piece of legal advice. "As far as I know, there is no law against mob violence," Flannigen said. What's more, police could not stop such violence, because they could not arrest everyone involved. Many in the crowd whooped and cheered at Flannigen's perilous argument.

Flannigen got just what he called for. A group of people rushed out of the hall after his speech, down the stairs, and onto the street. There they met the overspill crowd, which was quickly spreading rumors of race violence.

A black man had shot a white man during a robbery, according to one story being spread through the crowd. As rumors do, these stories changed with each retelling. People began saying the victim of the robbery had died, making the incident a murder. The victim became a white woman, then a woman with a girl, or two girls. The clash of details and the absence of any firsthand witnesses did not matter to the crowd.

A present-day photo of Collinsville Avenue in East St. Louis, where in
1917 white mobs attacked any black person they encountered

The mob assembled in front of the police station, where they watched for the "paddy wagon" that brought suspects to jail. When it arrived and police took out a black man in hand-cuffs, ringleaders of the mob began shouting that the prisoner was the man who had done the shooting. The most zealous vigilantes decided to take the situation in their own hands.

Groups of men ran down Collinsville Avenue, one of the main north-south streets in town. They attacked every black person they could find, pulling people off the sidewalk and knocking them to the ground. Those unfortunate enough to be caught were kicked and beaten mercilessly. The rioters stopped trolleys, went on board, and grabbed African American pas-sengers. The vigilantes grabbed one man, held him down on the trolley tracks and demanded that the trolley driver run him over. The driver refused, a brave act indeed in the face of an angry violent mob.

They stormed through the business district, attacking black bars, restaurants, and barber shops. They torched black homes. The owner of a pawnshop suspected of selling guns to black people held off the crowd with his own gun, threatening to shoot anyone who crossed his threshold. As news of the riot-ing spread, the crowd swelled to 3,000.

Mayor Mollman tried to get the Illinois National Guard to help put a stop to the riot, but he could not get anyone to give the order. The commanding officer in East St. Louis said he could not take action without Governor Frank Lowden's approval. Mollman stayed on the phone much of the night but could not reach the governor.

The police were ineffective in stopping the rioting. Some officers merely watched as the crowd ran amuck. Others acted with considerable courage. When a group of rioters tried to set a row of black homes on fire, detectives Samuel Coppedge and Frank Wodley held them off at gunpoint.

As black people warned one another and cleared the street, the rioters ran out of easy victims. At about two in the morning, one of the ringleaders told the others they might as well cease their bloodshed for the night. A newspaper later reported his words.

"Come on, fellows, let's go home," he said. "Tomorrow night we'll be ready for them. We are not armed now, but tomorrow we'll all have guns. We'll burn the negroes out and run them out of town."

Early the next morning, Mayor Mollman finally reached Governor Frank Lowden. The governor agreed to send National Guard troops. Mayor Mollman announced a series of measures to stop further rioting. Groups larger than five would be banned from the streets. Saloons, theaters, and schools would be closed until order was restored. The mayor imposed a ban on gun sales in the city as well.

Governor
Frank Lowden

Mayor Mollman also asked the mayor of St. Louis, which lay just across the river, to participate in the gun ban, but only to black people. St. Louis whites could still buy weapons. It was an odd decision, since black people had been the victims in the first night's rioting. Police searched African Americans and their vehicles far more often than they did whites.

The National Guard quelled the rioting the second night. Crowds of angry would-be rioters showed up downtown, where they met armed resistance. Even so, the vigilantes managed to inflict damage, beating black workers as they left factories and setting fire to black homes. But the guard's tactic of breaking up mobs gradually wore the rioters down. By midnight, most of them had cleared the streets.

The city had been lucky, at least in one sense. No one had died in the riots, despite the savage beatings. But the peace that followed was an uneasy one.

Flare-ups of racial violence continued throughout June. Attackers beat African Americans on trolleys and outside factories as workers finished their shifts. Some black employees began to carry guns. The police added to the hostility by enforcing the gun ban only against blacks, denying them the means to protect themselves.

The rage built up since the May riot exploded in July. It began with rumors of more violence. Early on the Sunday evening of July 1, a story spread of a black man shooting a white man in a fight. A black woman ran to a group of black men gathered at an intersection and told them that a white gang had attacked her and torn her dress. Some of the men wanted to seek out the gang and retaliate, but the more cautious among them advised against it.

Late that evening, a group of white men in a Model T Ford turned onto Market Street in South End, a neighborhood with several African American homes. They fired volleys of shots into houses, then quickly sped away. A bell rang at an African Methodist Episcopal church, and some people said afterwards that its tolling might have been a call to arms for the black population. The police department sent detectives Samuel Coppedge and Frank Wodley, the same officers who had protected black homes during the May riot, to investigate the shootings. They traveled to South End with uniformed police and a reporter. The police car was also a Model T Ford.

A Model T Ford automobile

The reporter was Roy Albertson of the *St. Louis Republic*. His published story of what happened next would play a large role in setting off the riot. What is certain is that the black crowd fired on the police, killing Coppedge and Wodley instantly and leaving their car riddled with bullet holes.

But Albertson's story made it seem as if the shooting of whites by blacks was an act of unprovoked malice. He downplayed the significance of the earlier attack by white shooters and claimed the detectives had even shown a badge to their African American attackers, a detail that seemed unlikely in the midst of an angry crowd that had gathered in an area with sparse streetlight. Albertson's story in the *St. Louis Republic* also claimed the slayings were the result of a prearranged slaughter. The story enraged many white readers. So did the sight of the police car, shot through with bullet holes, parked near the police station the next morning.

A little after nine on the morning of July 2, a meeting was held at the Labor Temple, a hall for union activities. Speakers urged the crowd to mount a violent response to the police shootings. After more than a month of rising racial tension, the listeners were all too ready to take revenge. They marched from the meeting hall in an orderly column, unhurried and calm, toward a streetcar transfer point on Broadway. They quickly shot a black man down in broad daylight, the first victim in what became a massacre.

From about 10:00 a.m. until early afternoon rioters attacked black homes and people in the street. They beat people, lynched people, and burned people alive in their houses. They set upon anyone who attempted to stop them and threatened anyone who tried to get them to show mercy. They made no distinction on the basis of gender or age, attacking men, women, and children. People acted almost like monsters, unleashing a buried and ugly sadism. Parents who ran out of their burning houses were shot dead along with their children, and their

African Americans walking on a sidewalk in East St. Louis,
Illinois, during the race riots of 1917

bodies thrown into the flames. The mob stoned some people to death. They attempted to prolong the suffering of their victims, beating and kicking them long after they had suffered lethal blows.

One newspaper reported "there was a horribly cool deliberateness and a spirit of fun about it." White boys as young as thirteen joined in the slaughter, as did young women armed with knives and broomsticks.

Eleven-year-old Freda Josephine McDonald lived with her family in a shack near downtown St. Louis. She never forgot the events of July 2. Years later, she wrote:

> An ominous humming sound filled the air.
>   It seemed to be drawing nearer.
> 'Is there a storm coming, Mama?'
>   my brother Richard asked.
> 'No, not a storm, child, it's the whites.'

Two years after the mob violence, McDonald, at age thirteen, left East St. Louis for the East coast. She later became known as Josephine Baker, the internationally famous entertainer and civil rights activist.

When ambulance drivers attempted to rescue victims, the mobs ran them off. White fire fighters met much the same fate, facing jeers and threats when they attempted to put out house fires. "Let 'em burn!" became the mob chant.

Afterwards, it was difficult to identify many of the bodies and to tally up the property damage. Death estimates ranged from forty-seven by a U.S. Congressional committee to two hundred, reported by the NAACP. The block between Broadway and Eighth streets was burned to the ground, along with forty-three houses on Bond Avenue between Tenth and Twelfth streets.

It was the deadliest race riot of the time, and it shocked not only St. Louis residents and officials, but black and white leaders all over the country. Marcus Garvey, one of the nation's most prominent black activists, blamed the mayor.

Marcus Garvey
in 1924

"I can not see where from Mayor Mollman got the authority to discourage black men going into East St. Louis, when there was work for them, except he got that authority from mob sentiment and mob law," Garvey said in a speech.

The United States Congress attempted to sort out the reasons for the gruesome violence with its own investigation. The legislators met in October and November of 1917 and held so many interviews that transcripts filled almost 5,000 pages. One of the more troubling findings came when the congressmen discovered they could not even set an accurate casualty count. Bodies had been dumped in the river, and no one was sure how many. Mobs burned some of their victims as well. To make matters worse, county officials did not even determine the cause of death for many of the bodies brought in during the riot.

The Congressional committee condemned the riots but did not do much else. It did not recommend that anyone be charged with any specific crime. Soldiers who had taken part faced no court-martials. As in other cases where cities failed to use the law to protect African Americans, thousands of black citizens of East St. Louis simply packed their belongings and left the city to seek freedom, economic security, and safety from violence somewhere else.

6

CHICAGO, 1919:
THE INVISIBLE LINE
OF COLOR

"One unidentified negro about 28 years old, riding a bicycle was waylaid by a mob of whites in Lyttle Street shortly after 9 o'clock tonight, stabbed and then shot sixteen times. When the unfortunate man fell from his bicycle apparently dead, some of the rioters poured gasoline over his body, which was then set afire. Policemen were rushed to the scene, extinguished the flames and took the charred body to the morgue. No arrests were made."

A *New York Times* report, published on July 30, 1919

Chicago stood at the American crossroads of prosperity and possibility in the early twentieth century. Chicagoans sometimes projected a rude, tough and ambitious image, but another side of the city was its diversity, born of its willingness to accept people of all races and national origin. One of its proudest residents was Carl Sandburg, who wrote a famous poem praising the city for its vitality and broad vision.

Carl Sandburg in 1955

Sandburg described the city this way:

> HOG Butcher for the World,
> Tool Maker, Stacker of Wheat,
> Player with Railroads and the Nation's Freight
> Handler;
> Stormy, husky, brawling,
> City of the Big Shoulders

Sandburg held another role besides that of poet in his job as a reporter for one of the city's daily newspapers. His poem *Chicago* described a city bold, unafraid, and brimming with youthful energy. As a reporter, he would have to describe an opposite side of the city to his readers—a side in which violence would erupt from fear of outsiders and from changing boundaries between black and white.

Black veterans pushed racial issues into the public light when they came home from World War I. Returning soldiers were eager to play their roles in the expansion of the nation. Young African American men saw an opportunity. If they fought for the country, wore its uniform and fired against its enemies, America would surely have to accept them as full citizens once they came home.

America's black soldiers thought they could end their legacy as slaves with their war sacrifice and make their way as full citizens thereafter. This belief would rank among the greatest disappointments in the African American struggle toward equality.

Instead of equality, black veterans found a country where little had changed. They may have considered World War I a watershed, but many white Americans saw the end of the war as merely a return to the status quo. In the cities, African Americans learned they were a separate society at best and an economic enemy to white workers at their worst. This new generation of black Americans grew more and more restless. Writers began referring to this young generation as the "New Negro," made up of African Americans who were less willing to settle for the rural lifestyle and less deferential to white people.

This gap between what young blacks expected from America and what they got helped to spark riots during what came to be called the Red Summer of 1919. Racial tension rose throughout the summer, fed by African American war veterans' resentment of unequal treatment, labor unrest, and competition for jobs. Before it was over, riots erupted in more than twenty American cities. Chicago would take the ignoble rank of the worst urban violence in the carnage.

America was caught in fear of another sort as well. In 1917, revolutionaries overthrew the czars of Russia, and went on to establish a Communist government. Many Americans feared

Revolutionaries attacking the czar's police during the first days of the
March Revolution of 1917 in Russia

the same thing would happen here. Some authorities linked any social reformers to the "Reds" who had led the Russian revolution. African Americans advocating for racial equality were lumped into that category.

The *New York Times* trumpeted the conspiracy theory in an article with the headline "REDS TRY TO STIR NEGROES TO REVOLT" that was filled with exaggerated claims of links between black publications and Communist radicals. J. Edgar Hoover, who would soon be the head of the FBI, thought African American leaders conspired with Communists.

In Chicago, there was no Communist conspiracy behind the riot. It was a seemingly small thing, a crossing of the nearly invisible color line.

The city appeared welcoming to many southern African Americans during the Great Migration, and on many fronts it was everything it seemed. Labor recruiters sought black workers for the meat-packing industry, among others. The work may have been nasty and hard, as meat-processing jobs of the early 1900s often were, but work was steady and pay was well above any comparable jobs in the South.

But the city also had a shadow side to its reputation as a refuge for those seeking to throw off the slave legacy. It threw its doors open to blacks workers in its factories, only to enforce unwritten rules of segregation in restaurants, trolleys, and public beaches. Housing also divided the races, with blacks and whites living in separate neighborhoods.

Chicago workers of different ethnic groups felt threatened by competition from African American arrivals. Meat-packers and other factory workers lived in fear of their wages being undercut by those recruited from down south. Black workers pouring into the train stations from Atlanta and Birmingham meant a tide of new arrivals who would take almost any wage for deliverance from the Jim Crow South.

The aspirations of the black war vets were higher than a job working for little pay. They had gone through the experiences of other ex-soldiers, including the pride of having carried a U.S. flag into battle against the enemy. They felt they were entitled to full American citizenship and lacked the patience of earlier generations whose experience was linked to shackles and forced labor. They had defended the country against its enemies and returned with optimistic visions of a changed world.

Newspapers in Chicago reported racial news in a manner not much more balanced than papers in the South. After the riot, Walter White of the NAACP took a look at the picture the city's journalists had portrayed of its black residents and found a mean-spirited journalism written to inspire hatred.

"Headlines such as 'Negro Brutally Murders Prominent Citizen,' 'Negro Robs House', and the like have appeared with alarming frequency and the news articles beneath such headlines have been of the same sort," White wrote.

"During the rioting such headlines as 'Negro Bandits Terrorize Town,' 'Rioters Burn 100 Homes—Negroes Suspected of Having Plotted Blaze' appeared." The newspapers carried every sort of wild exaggeration and rumor possible, spun so as to create the most lurid suspicions between both races. They carried tales of white women and children attacked and murdered, thrown from bridges, and subjected to almost every possible atrocity. They ruthlessly abused their responsibility as journalists in the never-ending campaign to drive their number of readers higher.

Many of the public places in Chicago were officially open to both races, but were actually segregated by unwritten rules observed by both races. So it was with the beaches. During the hot months, many Chicagoans packed the shore on Twenty-sixth and Twenty-ninth streets. But blacks stayed mostly on the beaches of Twenty-seventh streets, while whites flocked to Twenty-ninth Street.

The summer of 1919 was long and hot, and beaches swarmed with swimmers and people seeking to get out of their sweltering houses and apartments. One such beach-goer was Eugene Williams, a young black man. On the Sunday afternoon of July 27, Williams ventured offshore with several friends. Some of them swam, while Williams paddled a raft.

Trouble was already beginning as Williams swam out. A group of four African Americans walked through a crowd of white people on the Twenty-ninth Street beach. White men ordered them to leave, which they did. But they returned a little later, with more black men, and the two groups got into a stone-throwing fight.

As he headed farther out in the water, Williams crossed over to the white area of the beach. A white man took it on himself to enforce the color line and began hurling rocks at Williams. With the rock fight still rattling the beach, the boy could not return to shore. One of the stones struck him and knocked him from the raft. After clinging for a while to a railroad tie, Williams went down. Swimmers of both races tried to save him but failed. Williams drowned.

African Americans who had seen the tragedy were incensed. They complained to a white policeman that the stone thrower had caused Williams's death, but the officer refused to arrest him. When a white man made a complaint against a black man, the policeman swiftly arrested the black man. This was a dangerous arrest, given the angry mood of the crowd. The beach fights mushroomed into a mob fight, and the call went out for police reinforcements.

The first exchange of gunfire erupted about two hours later. When a group of police officers arrived at the beach, a black gunman fired into their midst. A black policeman fired back, and the gunman was shot dead. Violence grew worse after the sun set, as rumors of the drowning and shooting spread. Whites and blacks clashed in areas near the beach throughout the night. By sunup, twenty-seven people had been beaten, stabbed, or shot.

Most people returned to work the next morning, and it looked as if full-scale hostilities might be avoided. That hope vanished when African Americans began returning home on the streetcars. They met white mobs, who stopped the streetcars, dragged off black passengers, and savagely beat them.

Black people in Chicago had become used to a level of citizenship not common in the South, or even other cities in Illinois. They more aggressively defended themselves and counterattacked more than African Americans had in previous riots. When rumors spread that residents of an apartment building at Thirty-fifth Street and Wabash Avenue had killed a black man, a black mob surrounded the building. About a hundred police officers arrived and waded into the crowd. The bloody fighting left four dead.

White vigilantes raced into black neighborhoods, burning, looting, and terrorizing residents. Hospitals filled with the wounded. Rampaging rioters shut down trolleys and elevated streetcars. The telephone system went down as people cut phone wires.

The worst of the rioting went on for seven days. Street battles would flare up, play out their violent course, and an uneasy peace would temporarily prevail, only to ignite again a few blocks away or in a different part of town. A gunfight on July 28 claimed fourteen lives, when black and white gunmen sought the height of roof tops and upper-story windows to better aim as they fired upon their targets. The battle continued into the following day.

A white gang looking for blacks during the Chicago race riots of 1919

Many of the white rioters were very young men and boys, members of the white "athletic clubs," groups that were far more involved in street violence than athletics. They went by colorful names such as "Ragan's Colts," the "Hamburgers," and "Our Flag." These gangs showed cold-blooded ruthlessness, killing men, women, and children with equal enthusiasm. They even dismembered some of their victims.

A crowd of African American men standing on the sidewalks in front of a Walgreen Drugs in Chicago during the race riot. Police officers are standing at the forefront of the crowd.

It became a dangerous act to even drive a car down the street. Rioters pulled both white and black passengers from cars and beat them, often destroying the cars as well. Street cars and trolleys suffered much the same fate, until public transportation had to be halted on Forty-third, Forty-seventh, and Fifty-first streets.

The police were sometimes helpful in tamping down the violence, but many officers sympathized with white rioters and refused to arrest them. A reporter for the African American newspaper the *Defender* described a scene he had mostly witnessed while lying on his belly to avoid being shot.

"It occurred at Wabash avenue and 35th street at 8:10 o'clock at night, when over fifty policemen, mounted and on foot, while in the attempt to disperse a mob that was playing havoc with every white face, drew their revolvers and showered bullets into the crowd," the reporter wrote. "The officers' guns barked for fully ten minutes."

Hysteria on the part of some public officials led to greater public fear. An alderman told the *Daily News* that guerrilla war had broken out and bombs were going off. His account made it seem that police were on the verge of fleeing. "Frightened white men told me the police captains had just rushed through the district crying, 'For God's sake, arm; they are coming; we cannot hold them,'" he told the news reporter. But no evidence was ever found of a bomb going off.

A slow response to the riots by the state militia made the violence worse. The governor had sent the militia to the city on the second day of the riot, but Mayor William Hale Thompson continued to try to use the police to quell the rioting. Hale said he was afraid the young men of the militia would lack the experience and judgment to deal with such an event. About 2,800 of the city's 3,500 police officers were committed to the rioting. Even with those numbers on their side, they could not get the bloodshed under control.

Five policemen and one soldier with a rifle standing on a street corner during the 1919 race riot in the Douglas community of Chicago

On the fourth night, the mayor did dispatch the militia. They performed more ably than he had thought they would. The gunfights and street assaults gradually came to a halt. The rioting left twenty-three blacks and fifteen whites dead, more than five hundred injured, and a thousand people homeless.

Stunned public officials attempted to find reasons that so much violence had erupted so quickly in a city where blacks and whites had coexisted in a mostly peaceful fashion. "Prior to 1915, Chicago had been famous for its remarkably fair attitude toward colored citizens," wrote Walter White of the NAACP.

But the public response in the aftermath of the riots was not so fair. A grand jury convened, seeking to ferret out those responsible. It handed down seventeen indictments. All of them were against African Americans. The coroner's office examined 450 witnesses to prepare its Coroner's Report of 1919, which blamed the riot on social and economic conditions.

President Woodrow Wilson surprised some of his critics. He had long been regarded with suspicion by African American leaders, because of such things as his southern roots and his sympathy for the Confederate cause in the Civil War. But Wilson blamed whites for their participation in the violence and came out in favor of voluntary organizations to deal with racial relations. But the president proposed no fundamental changes in the laws that made African Americans second-class citizens. He also left intact the segregation of the races that was one of the hallmarks of his administration.

Walter White summed it up simply. He used now outmoded language for members of his race, but solid reasoning, when he concluded his report on the violence. "Colored men saw their own kind being killed, heard of many more and believed that their lives and liberty were at stake," he wrote. "In such a spirit most of the fighting was done."

Many homes were vandalized during the riots. These photos show militia standing guard as white onlookers congregate in front of some of the destroyed houses.

The Red Summer

"The Red Summer" is a phrase attributed to James Weldon Johnson, the distinguished Harlem Renaissance writer, lawyer, diplomat, journalist, song writer, and civil rights activist who served as the first black president of the NAACP. Black American soldiers had helped the U.S. win the war for worldwide "democracy" during World War I, and when they returned to America they expected their share of "democracy." Instead, many found themselves at "war" with white Americans determined to return the soldiers to their prewar status, which was at the bottom of American society. This prompted Johnson to say, "Eight months after the armistice, with black men back fresh from the front, there broke the Red Summer of 1919, and the mingled emotions of the race were bitterness, despair, and anger." Johnson's words, the Red Summer, have been interpreted different ways over the years. Some have said red refers to the blood of the black people killed during the six-month rash of violence from April to early October in 1919. Others have said it refers to the spilled blood of all who died, black and white. Still others have speculated that it referenced the red of the Red Scare of 1919-1920, following the Russian Revolution.

7

TULSA, 1921: BLOOD ON "BLACK WALL STREET"

"Oh lawdy, me . . . . My house burned, my clothes burned, my chickens burned. Nothing have I but the clothes on my back! Oh lawdy, that I should live to see such a day."
An unidentified elderly African American woman

Residents of Tulsa, Oklahoma, called it "the Magic City." Technological and economic wonders had transformed it from a backwards small town to a rising urban center of the state. Much of Tulsa's economic strength came from the oil fields discovered in 1905. As one refinery after another went up, shops and service businesses expanded to serve customers with newfound wealth.

African Americans joined in the spoils, not always the case in rapidly developing cities. The Greenwood section north of the city center of Tulsa became known as the "Black Wall Street," because of the relative wealth enjoyed by its residents. Entrepreneurs prospered in Greenwood, with theaters, grocery stores, and shops springing up as black Tulsans applied the American lessons of free enterprise.

Not everyone in Greenwood was rich, of course. Rows of simple frame houses that belonged to the lower working classes stood not far from the larger homes of the well-to-do. But the section had so many nice places where people could shop and entertain themselves that it became a favorite destination of people who lived in poorer districts.

Tolerance and acceptance followed in the wake of prosperity. Tulsa had enough wealth to go around, and work was plentiful. Most Tulsans wanted to live and let live. Unfortunately, there were those who held suspicions of any people who were not white, Anglo-Saxon Protestants.

A movement called "nativism" gained momentum during World War I. Nativism claimed America's real strength came from the European settlers of Colonial times. All other races and more recent immigrants were to be rejected. The war provided a perfect excuse for those who believed in such ideas to carry them out on a national level. In the name of patriotism, people took out their fears and suspicion on anything or anyone German. They renamed sauerkraut as "liberty cabbage" and banned the performance of German music. Even the owners of dachshunds, a German breed of dog, had to watch their pets carefully, for some overzealous "patriots" took their hatred to the level of animal abuse.

Nativist arguments appealed to the Ku Klux Klan, as well as other bigoted societies. The Klan targeted Jews, Catholics, and African Americans, as being among those not "American"

The Ku Klux Klan was very active in Oklahoma.

enough to deserve the full rights of citizenship. The KKK was clandestine by nature, and no one is sure how many Klansmen lived in Tulsa prior to the riot. But in the years following the violence, Oklahoma became a hotbed of Klan activity.

Prejudice in the media added fuel to the dangerous mix. Greenwood was fortunate enough to have not only a black newspaper, but two of them, the *Tulsa Star* and the *Tulsa Sun*. Neither of them was a match in terms of opinion-making for the outspoken and racist publisher of the *Tulsa Tribune*, Richard Lloyd Jones.

Jones was a son of a wealthy Wisconsin family. He bought the *Tulsa Democrat* in 1919 and changed the name to the *Tribune*. Jones was a tall, aristocratic looking man who wore expensive suits, kept his spacious office filled with books, and idolized President Lincoln. Jones's infatuation with Lincoln

Richard Lloyd Jones in his office at the *Tulsa Tribune*

was more than a little ironic, since few in the media hated or distrusted African Americans more than Jones. His office was near the Greenwood section, but he never stopped resenting the residents there.

Jones's editorials were filled with rage and venom. Tulsa had all the crime problems of any growing city, including drugs, prostitution, and gambling. Jones was quick to blame black people for most of these ills. He threw caution aside when filling his pages with stories casting suspicion and blame on black Tulsans. On top of it, he liberally sprinkled his articles with racial slurs.

In the spring of 1921, Jones's bigotry found a natural target, in the form of a story about an alleged crime by a young black man against a white woman. As often in the course of racial violence, this incident inflamed the imaginations of those who always feared the worst from African American men.

Dick Rowland worked shining shoes on the ground floor of the Drexel Building. Rest room facilities were still segregated, and the only black rest room stood on the fourth floor. Rowland became at least somewhat acquainted with Sarah Page, the operator for the one elevator in the building. That is all the information anyone knew for sure about their relationship, for the details of the story of Rowland and Page became much disputed after the events of May 30, 1921.

Rowland rode Page's elevator up to the fourth floor, used the facilities, and got back on. On the ride back down, something happened in the elevator. What happened has never been fully revealed. When the elevator door opened, Rowland hurried out. Page was crying, distraught and her clothing was disheveled. When a white man who worked in the building asked what had happened, she told him Rowland had raped her. Rowland told a different story, saying he had grabbed her arm when he momentarily lost his footing. Police arrested Rowland the morning after the incident.

On May 31, the *Tulsa Tribune* ran a lurid story with the headline "Nab Negro for Attacking Girl in Elevator." The headline meant police had "nabbed" or caught the attacker. It identified Rowland as "Diamond Dick," a nickname he sometimes used, and called Page "an orphan who works as an elevator operator to pay her way through business college." Predictably, the story enraged white readers.

The story came out in the afternoon edition of the *Tribune*. By seven o'clock on the evening of May 31, a crowd of nearly eight hundred people had gathered outside the courthouse. People were already talking about a lynching.

African Americans did not take lynching threats lightly, and they knew Rowland was in great danger of physical harm from the charges against him and the way they had been reported. A group of men met in the office of the *Tulsa Star* in Greenwood, trying to decide the best course of action. About thirty of them got in their cars and drove to the courthouse. There they offered their help to Sheriff W. M. "Bill" McCullough to prevent Rowland's being lynched. McCullough knew as well as they did the danger to his prisoner and had already moved him to the top floor of the jail to take Rowland as far as possible from the growing crowd. The sheriff had also turned several white men away when they tried to enter the jail. He told the Greenwood men that he did not need their help.

More Greenwood residents arrived throughout the evening. As in the Chicago riot of 1919, many of them were veterans who had fought in World War I. The idea of fighting for their country, only to come home to violence against their race, angered these former soldiers. Soon there were two crowds at the courthouse, one white and one black. It did not take long for the initial spark that triggered the riot. Someone fired a single shot. An eruption of gunfire lit up the faces in the crowd, and everyone cleared the streets to take cover.

The fear and rage unleashed in those first minutes of the riot later blurred the details for some survivors. Everyone agreed that someone had been shot dead in the first cross fire. Papers reported the death, but accounts were so unreliable, they could not even agree on the race of the victim.

People began breaking into closed hardware stores, seeking guns and ammunition. Rioters attempted to break into the National Guard Armory but did not succeed. The guardsmen held them off.

Part of the mob ran through the streets, searching for any black person they could find, savagely beating those unlucky enough to fall into their hands. Others mounted an attack with more deadly efficiency. War veterans used their military training to organize into well-disciplined groups. The militia and other authorities referred to the "Negro uprising" and planned to crush it with force.

African Americans saw the riot as one more example of the mob violence they had suffered so many times when they seemed on the verge of successfully creating a niche for themselves in a city. Men in Greenwood also fell back on their military training. They grabbed up old service revolvers and rifles, along with helmets that had once protected them from German bullets as they fought in Europe.

Others were not so battle hardened as to be ready for outbursts of random violence. When the mobs ran them out of their houses, they emerged in nightclothes or barefooted. Such people were defenseless against rioters who sought to take everything from their possessions to their lives.

The police made disastrous mistakes in their reaction to the violence. They deputized men who were little more than street thugs in the attempt to put down the "uprising." These instant deputies more often than not used their authority as an unlimited license to murder, burn, and pillage. The police freely handed out guns as loaners. In many cases, that was the last they saw of the weapons.

White rioters descended upon the Greenwood district of Tulsa late in the evening hours of May 31, 1921. The rioting that ensued left much of the district in ruins and more than three hundred people dead.

The wave of violence rolled on for six hours. A skirmish line developed along the Frisco railroad tracks that divided Greenwood from the white part of town. African Americans held off the vigilantes and succeeded for a while in protecting their community. But rioters broke through the line of defenders and entered Greenwood in sufficient numbers to kill, torch, and murder in the first night of rioting.

Mob members poured into the neighborhood of one of Greenwood's most prized entertainment venues, the Dreamland theater. The theater was the property of a local black entrepreneur who started out as an automobile mechanic and went on to build enough wealth to run several businesses. Greenwood's residents flocked to the theater during their leisure time, forking over the fifteen cents admission to watch silent movies with casts of almost entirely white stars. A movie had just started when the manager got word of the mob gathering on the streets. He had the lights turned on and quickly cleared the theater.

Fires blazed in Greenwood throughout the night. Carloads of men drove through the section, firing randomly into houses. Rumors of an African American counterattack rippled through the mob throughout the night, even though the Greenwood combatants were doing well to even defend their neighborhood. The National Guard did a much better job of protecting rioters than Greenwood residents. The Guard had bought into the notion that the battle was a one-sided black "uprising." They treated all the Greenwood men captured like prisoners of war, marching them in columns to the city Convention Center.

The riot went into a brief lull during the hours between three and five in the morning. The rioters regrouped and made plans for a hard assault the next day. Greenwood residents woke up to the sound of whistles blowing and men shouting as the second wave of rioters descended upon them.

Tulsa, 1921

The National Guard was called in to enforce martial law in Greenwood.

As the day dawned, people looked out their windows and peered from hiding places to see a mob working far more methodically than it had in its first frenzy. Rioters would invade a house, send the women and children out, and then "arrest" the men. If anyone resisted, the vigilantes murdered them. They then looted the house of clothes, musical instruments, furniture, and anything else of remotest value. Finally they set fire to the house.

It became clear to almost everyone in Greenwood that the motive of their attackers had changed from the previous evening. They were no longer seeking mere retaliation for the courthouse clash, or even to put down any so-called uprising. The rioters wanted to burn out Greenwood residents and drive them out of town.

Fire trucks hurtled into the massacre, only to meet jeering mobs that would not let them through to the houses. The hooligans refused to even let them set up their hoses.

The usual atrocities linked with race riots happened once again in Tulsa. Accounts varied greatly, since newspapers were biased and witnesses scared for their lives. But people later came forward with grisly tales of armed roughnecks taking advantage of the weakest of victims. When one of his captors jabbed a rifle in the ribs of a man marching to be jailed, the black man angrily turned on him and was shot dead in the instant. Those marching behind the prisoners shot at their feet. A group of rioters savagely beat a crippled man who sold pencils downtown, then dragged him to death behind their car. The riot in Greenwood's residential area looked like a scene from hell, with looters laughing, dancing, and playing stolen musical instruments in the streets as houses burned.

One final strange twist set the Tulsa riot apart from those that came before it. The leaders of the riot commandeered planes, once again following the veterans' experience in the recent war. The planes shadowed the mob and dipped low over skirmish lines where whites and blacks clashed. Some said the pilots provided reconnaissance reports or watched for the approach of any African Americans from outside the city. Others said they dropped nitroglycerin, a powerful explosive, into the flames. The dispute over the planes' role continues to the present day, a result of the city's past leaders attempt to cloak their most shameful days in secrecy.

Whatever weapons were used to create the inferno, the city's "Black Wall Street" was no more by day's end. In its place lay acres of smoking black ash.

In the aftermath of the riot, people struggled to make sense of it. Some of the killers and looters would brag about it for the rest of their lives. Ku Klux Klansmen who took part were proud too, though, none wore their robes that night. But many decent citizens shared a sense of shame. Even newspapers that had spread race hatred called for an investigation.

A grand jury took up the task of trying to find reasons for the riot that had destroyed so much and cost so many lives. Its conclusions were yet another affront to the victims. The *Tulsa World* summed it up with a headline in late June: "Grand Jury Blames Negroes for Inciting Race Rioting; Whites Clearly Exonerated."

The report downplayed the threat of lynching by the white mob. All responsibility for the riot was to be born by the group of black men who showed up at the courthouse in an attempt to protect Dick Rowland. The real culprits were outside agitators who "had led (African Americans) as a people to believe in equal rights, social equality, and their ability to demand the same."

For most of the twentieth century, Tulsa buried the history of the riots. Newspapers and magazines would occasionally publish stories about it, but most Tulsans did not want to talk about so shameful a chapter in their history. Even so, stories by survivors continued to churn up details.

The Tulsa Tribune.

TULSA, OKLAHOMA, THURSDAY, JUNE 2, 1921.   City Edition * * *   TWELVE

XVII—NUMBER 236.

STRICT MARTIAL LAW LII

MARTIN BLAMES RIOTS TO LAX CITY HALL RULE

Fixes Responsibility, Plans Restoration

Scenes of Flame–Swept Black Belt

JURY INQUIRY IS DEMANDED BY GOVERNOR

Asks Quiz of Police and Sheriff

SEARCH CUTS KNOWN DEATH LIST TO 27

Nine Whites, Eighteen Blacks Found

The Dead

The Tulsa Tribune

Free Interned Negr
Red Cross Is in Cho

Scenes of destruction from the 1921 riot

TED

CITY WILL BE
OPEN TONIGHT
BARRETT SAYS

Guardsmen Still Rule
Trouble District

In 1997, the Oklahoma state legislature set up a commission to study the riot in detail. Legislator Don Ross sponsored a bill to pay reparations of $5 million total to survivors. The commission indeed recommended payment of reparations. But the state and city declined to pay the money. A federal court ruled that too much time had passed to expect governments to right the matter.

During the investigation, Ross described what he considered a terrible miscarriage of justice against early twentieth century Tulsa's most productive citizens. With three elderly survivors in attendance, he addressed a press conference.

"We told these people to lift themselves up by their bootstraps," he said. "And they did, forming the most successful black community in America. And once they had lifted themselves up by their bootstraps, we destroyed them for it."

8

DETROIT, 1943: WRECKING AMERICA'S ARSENAL

"Our . . . [race riot] in 1943 was the worst thing I've ever seen. People killed like flies. I went down on Alfred and Hastings Street, picked up a man down there that the police just took an automatic gun and . . . cut him in two. You had to pick up one part of him and then pick up another part. I shipped him back to his home in Mississippi."
M. Kelly Fritz, a black funeral home owner

In 1943, Detroit was a factory city with a proud sense of its own history. Henry Ford had started his Ford Motor Company there in 1903. Ford did not invent the automobile, but he created the assembly lines that kept Detroit factories churning out his famed black Model-T cars by the thousands. The name of the city would become a media nickname for the American automotive industry, much as "Wall Street" refers to the stock market.

In the World War II era, Detroit earned a different tag: the "Arsenal of Democracy." Adolf Hitler's armies had started the war in 1939 with Germany's invasion of Czechoslovakia, but many Americans were initially reluctant to enter the war. The United States would not declare war until late 1941, after the December 7 bombing of Pearl Harbor by Japan, an ally of Germany. But by 1940, Germany's relentless bombing of London had convinced President Franklin Delano Roosevelt that America would probably have to fight as well.

Roosevelt set a goal of producing 50,000 planes per year, a daunting task for any nation at the time. Detroit's know-how helped make this goal a reality. California plants turned out planes at about one per day at the time the war started. By using the assembly-line technology, Detroit plants soon rolled out a plane an hour as well.

Roosevelt was not the first person to call Detroit the "Arsenal of Democracy," but he helped make it a household term. The president used those words in his "fireside chats," radio broadcasts he used to bolster the nation's morale.

The president also worked with civil rights leaders on the war effort, to a degree that was rare in those days. With the war on his shoulders, Roosevelt did not see African American rights as a top priority. A. Philip Randolph forced President Roosevelt's hand. Randolph, an African American labor leader who was president of the Brotherhood of Sleeping Car Porters, threatened a march on Washington in 1941 if Roosevelt did not ban discrimination against blacks in defense industry jobs. Roosevelt yielded to Randolph's pressure and signed an executive order prohibiting racial discrimination in defense plants.

In theory, black workers in Detroit's plane factories were now entitled to every benefit due white coworkers. But Detroit had a troubled history of race relations.

A. Philip Randolph in 1942

In the 1920s, the Ku Klux Klan had taken hold in the city, and it remained strong there through the war years. Detroit held to a system of segregation that kept blacks and whites apart in everything from restaurants and shops to residential areas. Whites and blacks did not mix or know one another for the most part, and as always with segregation, ignorance led to suspicion. Police did not trust African Americans, and black citizens returned the distrust.

But with war quotas looming, the factories desperately needed workers. As with other northern cities, plants in Detroit sent recruiters south to recruit workers. The pay was good, and work was plentiful. Yet the factories did not provide housing. Eventually, most of the city's working class African Americans settled into a sixty-square block ghetto, without adequate sanitation. Ironically, the name of the neighborhood was Paradise Valley.

In 1941, the Detroit Housing Commission set up two housing projects, one white and the other black. The black project was named Sojourner Truth, after the African American poet of Civil War times. But when the project was complete, nearby white residents became enraged that black residents would move into the neighborhood. The threat of violence was so great, the houses sat empty for months after being completed in late September.

In February of 1942, the first black families signed leases and attempted to move into Sojourner Truth. They met 150 residents who formed a picket line and set a cross on fire in the style of the Klan. The intimidation worked, at least at first, and the blacks stayed out. But on the second day of the picket, two black men tried to run a car through the picket line. Fighting became so intense that mounted police fired tear gas into the crowd. Violence continued off and on until April, when black families finally settled into the homes they had leased in the winter. With frequent outbursts of random violence, tensions simmered for a year before exploding at Belle Isle.

A sign posted outside of the Sojourner Truth housing project in 1942

Belle Isle was a huge island amusement park located on the Detroit River, popular among both races. It was crowded on the Sunday night of June 20, 1943, and recent racial friction had some of the crowd spoiling for a fight. Small fistfights broke out between whites and blacks, most of them teens, throughout the evening.

As the crowd began to return home that evening, traffic jams kept cars moving slowly. More fights erupted and grew larger as tempers flared. Sailors from the nearby Naval Armory were notorious fighters, and they joined the hostilities. The fistfights began to turn into a fighting mob, and before long, about two hundred sailors took their parts. Soon the mob was attacking anyone who was black and chasing people who were on foot. A crowd of whites gathered at the point where the bridge joined the mainland, cutting off black motorists. As word spread of the battle on the bridge, people on the mainland side joined in and the crowd swelled to about 5,000. It was midnight before police cars arrived at the bridge, far too late to quell the growing race rage.

Rumors of the bridge fight made it sound even worse than it was. The trouble in Paradise Valley erupted from a bar called the Forest Club. A black man who identified himself as a policeman went into the club and told the late night patrons that whites had thrown an African American woman over the bridge and her child in after her. Angry blacks left the club seeking vengeance for the reported atrocity. They did not know of an equally ugly rumor among whites, spreading the tale that a black man had raped and killed a white woman.

Both rumors caused white and black mobs to form and carry out acts of vengeance. The black rioters swarmed the streets of Paradise Valley, seeking white drivers, pedestrians, and white-owned businesses. They beat people with fists and rocks, yanking them from their cars and into the streets.

They set upon a bus carrying white workers home from the factory and stoned white riders. Looting followed in the wake of the attacks, with store windows smashed and groceries, liquor, and dry goods stolen.

A white mob formed outside the Roxy, an African American theater. When moviegoers left the Roxy, they faced groups of angry whites who surrounded and savagely beat them. When they saw cars driven by blacks, they rocked the cars until they toppled upside down and set them on fire. Once again, workers got caught in the cross fire, as streetcars carrying black workers ran a gauntlet of angry whites. Victims began arriving at the city's Receiving Hospital so quickly that the staff was hard-pressed to treat them.

By three in the morning, a report went into the police department that the riot was out of control. Some officers shared in the blame, as they only watched the violence from their squad cars. A man at the Roxy urged the police to form escorts for people leaving the theater. An officer told him they could do nothing without orders from the police chief. Shortly thereafter, however, police did enter the theater and warned the people inside to stay put until protection could be arranged for them. Many officers did attempt to do their duty and went in harm's way. The rioters shot six policemen and injured seventy-five.

Shortly after four in the morning, the police commissioner called an emergency meeting. An agent of the FBI attended, as did top officers of the Michigan State Police, the Wayne County Sheriff's Department, and a colonel from the U.S. Army. But the meeting produced no effective plan of action and deadlocked on the question of whether to call for federal troops.

Early Monday morning an African American delegation met with the mayor, Edward Jeffries Jr., and urged him to call for federal troops. The mayor thought local authorities could handle the situation but called for another meeting later in the day to assess the danger.

A few citizens took it on themselves to act. The Detroit Citizens Committee handed out pamphlets urging the public to call off the riots. Reverend Horace White, an African American Congregational minister, rode through the streets of Paradise Valley in a truck equipped with a mounted loudspeaker. Residents awoke to the echoes of White's mobile sermon, calling on them to make peace.

But there would be no peace anytime soon. Even by noon, mobs were attacking people of the opposite race, and cars still blazed in the street. Drivers who did make it through looked out their windows to see savage beatings going on all around them. A reporter from the *Detroit News* attempted to get a story on the riot and almost did not make it past a group of assailants determined to make him the next casualty. Policemen saved him from the mob. Other officers, either because of frayed nerves or racism, did not act so admirably. Some bodies recovered from the street had police bullets in their backs.

Mounted police officers patrol near the Sojourner Truth housing project.

Even attempted acts of mercy proved deadly. An Italian doctor trying to make a house call in a black neighborhood was stoned and beaten to death by the mob.

Attempts to bring the riot under control backfired. The city dismissed high school students early in the afternoon, only to see them join the riot. Looting continued throughout the afternoon, with prime targets being any store that carried fresh meat or tavern with a supply of alcohol. Two black teachers attempting to drive home stalled their car in the parking lot and nearly paid with their lives when white students chopped through the car roof with axes. Police stopped the attempted murder. Other victims were not so lucky. A cab driver ran down and killed a white pedestrian. Four white teens attacked a black man waiting for a bus and stoned him to death.

The crowd in the northern downtown district swelled to 10,000. Whites marched into the black neighborhood, where they met a small army of angry African Americans. Paradise Valley homeowners stood armed by their doors and windows, and a few fired at the invading crowds. Not everyone who first joined in such marches had the stomach for the violence that resulted. Some people pulled back to retreat or watch, while the most violent on each side clashed. More frequently, gangs picked out single victims, the elderly, women, and children.

Some people who might not have ordinarily been prone to violence got caught up in the mob spirit. One of four teens who shot a black man admitted later that they had done the deed randomly and somewhat out of boredom. "We didn't know him," he said. "He wasn't bothering us. But other people were fighting and killing and we felt like it, too."

Late that day, Mayor Jeffries took a cautious tour through the city to survey the damage. Everywhere he went he saw carnage, violence, and vandalism. Burning cars littered the streets. At police barricades, officers were out-manned and out-gunned by rioters. Even tear gas was not enough to disperse them.

White gangs overturned and burned twenty cars belonging to blacks during the riots.

He decided finally to do what the African American delegation had asked him to do early that morning. He joined Governor Harry Kelly in calling on President Roosevelt to send in federal troops.

Governor Kelly declared martial law, banned liquor sales, and shut down public entertainment. The president dispatched 6,000 federal troops to Detroit. Once the army arrived, the riot ebbed, and the streets at last became safe for the most part. Yet for days afterward, random fights and attacks still occasionally flared up.

The city paid dearly in lives lost, injuries, and property ruined. In thirty-six hours, thirty-four people died, twenty-five of them black. Jails swelled even more than hospitals, with 1,800 people arrested.

Chaos erupts as a crowd of rioters estimated to be
in the thousands takes to the streets.

African American men, one with a bloodied eye, stand near police armed with clubs.

Naturally, the event caused terrible damage to the city's reputation. With a war on, the infamy did not stop at America's shores. In Germany, Nazi propagandists seized on the riot to report that Americans could not even keep the peace in the city in its highly praised "Arsenal of Democracy."

Nazi radio stations in France, which had fallen to Germany, denounced America as "a country torn by social injustice, race hatreds, regional disputes, the violence of an irritated proletariat, and the gangsterism of a capitalistic police." No one could deny the Detroit riots had damaged the international reputation of both the nation and the city.

Harsh feelings ran too strong, though, for any quick solution to Detroit's race problem. The behavior of the police during the riot worsened already strained relations with the African American community. Of the twenty-five black people who died, seventeen were killed by the police. The police did not kill any of the nine white people in the casualty count. All had died at the hands of other rioters.

Wayne County prosecutor William E. Dowling shifted the blame from the police to black rioters. He blamed the black press, the African American community, and even the National Association for the Advancement of Colored People for the bloodshed.

Dowling held an especially contemptuous view of the NAACP. When he sat on a mayor's council investigating the causes of the riot, he was astonished to hear a black reverend saying he had turned over his own accounts of the event to the association. He flew into a rage and had a table-pounding shouting fit at the preacher, telling him the NAACP should be indicted by a grand jury.

The prosecutor issued the "Dowling report," which blamed the riot on a "group of young Negro hoodlums." The report exonerated not only white rioters, but the police as well. It said the "ordinary law enforcement and judicial agencies have thus far dealt adequately and properly with the law violaters." Resulting rage in the black community was such that some African Americans who had witnessed the riots passed a distrust of the police down to their own sons and daughters, complicating race relations for years to come.

Optimists in the ranks of racial activists had hoped President Roosevelt would take the opportunity to seriously address the nation's problems on race. Perhaps he would give them some notice in his "fireside chats." But there would be no fireside chat about the violence in Detroit. The president's advisors warned him that he had much to gain and little to lose if he took the problem head-on. He could lose political support in his own party, particularly in the southern states where the Democratic Party was strong.

The president's only remarks were a tepid apology that framed the riot in terms of a tragedy without offering solutions. In a publicized letter to a New York congressman, Roosevelt wrote, "I share your feeling that the recent outbreaks of violence in widely scattered parts of the country endanger our national unity and comfort our enemies. I am sure that every true American regrets them." It seemed precious little to offer people who had helped make Detroit the world's most productive plane making city in America's most dangerous war.

Race riots leave memories and scars on cities that can overshadow their greatest achievements. Of course, they leave many dead and wounded. But they also divide and damage mutual interests. Violence tears down financial gains, particularly for those trying to climb the economic ladder. It destroys property. Bloodshed leaves its stain on cities for years afterward.

As the twentieth century passed its midpoint, race relations began to change in America, mostly for the better. The rise of the Civil Rights Movement gave African Americans greater equality in every sphere of life. Civil rights leaders, particularly Dr. Martin Luther King Jr., used nonviolent means to achieve their ends.

Yet, even King cautioned that "the more we find individuals facing conditions of frustration, conditions of disappointment and seething despair as a result of the slow pace of things and the failure to change conditions, the more it will be possible for the apostles of violence to interfere."

Sources

CHAPTER 1: A History of Violence

p. 10,   "If the black man . . ." Robert Thomas Kerlin, *The Voice of the Negro 1919*
          (New York: E. P. Dutton & Company, 1920), 128.

CHAPTER 2: Wilmington, 1898: A Democracy Overthrown

p. 17,   "Send relief . . ." LeRae Sikes Umfleet, *A Day of Blood: The 1898
          Wilmington Race Riot* (Raleigh, N.C.: North Carolina Office of Archives
          and History, in association with the African American Heritage
          Commission, 2009), 130.

p. 21,   "While we dealt . . . " "The North Carolina Election of 1898—Furnifold
          Simmons," http://www.lib.unc.edu/ncc/1898/bios/simmons.html.

p. 22,   "If it takes lynching . . ." "New Georgia Encyclopedia: Rebecca Latimer
          Felton (1835-1930)," http://www.georgiaencyclopedia.org/nge/Article.
          jsp?id=h-904.

p. 22,   "our experience teaches us . . . " "The Wilmington Record editorial—
          North Carolina Digital History," http://www.learnnc.org/lp/editions/
          nchist-newsouth/4363.

p. 23,   "choke the current of . . . " "How The Only Coup D'Etat of U.S.
          History Unfolded: NPR," http://www.npr.org/templates/story/story.
          php?storyId=93615391.

p. 23,   "perhaps the bloodiest race . . ." "North Carolina History Project: Alfred
          Moore Waddell (1834-1912)," http://www.northcarolinahistory.org/
          encyclopedia/97/entry.

p. 24,   "did not anticipate the enfranchisement . . . " North Carolina Office of
          Archives and History, "1898 Wilmington Race Riot Commission," http://
          www.history.ncdcr.gov/1898-wrrc/report/Chapter4.pdf.

p. 24,   "by means of their votes . . . " Ibid.

p. 25,   "so vile and slanderous . . . " Ibid., 77.

p. 26,   "no way responsible for, nor . . . " David S. Cecelski and Timothy B. Tyson,
          eds. *Democracy Betrayed: The Wilmington Race Riot of 1898 and Its
          Legacy*, "We Have Taken a City: A Centennial Essay," H. Leon Prather Sr.
          (University of North Carolina Press: Chapel Hill, London), 31.

p. 28,   "Now you have performed . . ." Umfleet, *A Day of Blood: The 1898
          Wilmington Race Riot*, 86.

p. 30,   "as few of the negroes . . ." Ibid, 88.

p. 30,   "[T]oday, we are mourners . . ." Umfleet, *A Day of Blood: The 1898
          Wilmington Race Riot*, 130.

p. 30,   "[A]re we do die . . ." Ibid.

p. 34,   "In many African traditions . . ." "Healing Art-KSU Prof's Art Helps Heal
          Racial Wounds," Kennesaw State University, http://web.kennesaw.edu/
          news/stories/healing-arts.

CHAPTER 3: Atlanta, 1906: Politics in a Powder Keg

p. 35,   "In the flickering light . . ." Walter Francis White, *A Man Called White: The Autobiography of Walter White* (New York: Viking Press, 1948), 11.

p. 40,   "When he turned . . ." Mark Bauerlein, *Negrophobia: A Race Riot in Atlanta, 1906* (San Francisco: Encounter Books, 2001), 124.

p. 41,   "NEGRO ATTEMPTS TO . . ." Ibid, 142.

p. 41,   "Come on, honey, . . ." Ibid, 143.

p. 41,   "SECOND ASSAULT," Ibid.

p. 41,   "THIRD ASSAULT," Ibid.

p. 44,   "Son, don't shoot until . . ." "Defending Home and Hearth: Walter White Recalls the 1906 Atlanta Race Riot," http://historymatters.gmu.edu/d/104/.

p. 47,   "a frightful carnival . . ." Gregory Mixon, *The Atlanta Riot: Race, Class and Violence in a New South City* (Gainesville, Florida: University Press of Florida, 2005), 120.

p. 47,   "straighten [himself] out . . ." Ibid, 121.

p. 50,   "Is this Thy Justice . . ." W. E. B. Du Bois, "Darkwater; voices from within the veil," http://etext.lib.virginia.edu/etcbin/toccer-new2id=DubDark. xml&images=images/modeng&data=/texts/english/modeng/parsed&tag=public&part=3&division=div1.

CHAPTER 4: Springfield, 1908: Murder in the City of Lincoln

p. 51,   "I ain't got . . ." Roberta Senechale de la Roche, *In Lincoln's Shadow: The 1908 Race Riot in Springfield, Illinois* (Carbondale: Southern Illinois University Press, 2008), 124.

p. 54,   "DRAGGED FROM HER BED . . ." "The Springfield Race Riot of 1908," http://library.thinkquest.org/2986/.

p. 55,   "If a cyclone had passed . . ." Carole Merritt, "Something So Horrible: The Springfield Race Riot of 1908," http://www.alplm.org/events/aa_history/ Race_Riot_Catalog_2008.pdf.

p. 58,   "They say my uncle . . ." Senechale de la Roche, *In Lincoln's Shadow: The 1908 Race Riot in Springfield, Illinois*, 139.

CHAPTER 5: East St. Louis, 1917: Worker Against Worker

p. 63,   "What I saw before me . . ." Harper Barnes, *Never Been a Time: The 1917 Race Riot that Sparked the Civil Rights Movement* (New York: Walker & Company, 2008), 144.

p. 66,   "Negro and cheap foreign labor . . ." Elliott M. Rudwick, *Race Riot at East St. Louis: July 2, 1917* (Carbondale, Il.: Southern Illinois University Press, 1964), 27-28.

p. 67,   "As far as I know . . ." Barnes, *Never Been a Time: The 1917 Race Riot That Sparked the Civil Rights Movement*, 99-100.

p. 70,   "Come on, fellows, let's . . ." Rudwick, *Race Riot at East St. Louis: July 2, 1917*, 30.

p. 74,   "there was a horribly cool . . . " "Digitization Projects Philologic Results," from Ida B. Wells-Barnett, *The East St. Louis Massacre: The Greatest Outrage of the Century* (Chicago: The Negro Fellowship Herald Press, 1917), http://lincoln.lib.niu.edu/cgi-bin/philologic/getobject.pl?c.5065:3.lincoln.

p. 74,   "An ominous humming . . ." Barnes, *Never Been a Time: The 1917 Race Riot that Sparked the Civil Rights Movement*, 143.

p. 75,   "Let 'em burn!" Ibid.

p. 76,   "I can not see where . . ." "American Experience | Marcus Garvey | Primary Sources," PBS.org, http://www.pbs.org/wgbh/amex/garvey/filmmore/ps_riots.html.

CHAPTER 6: Making the Case: the Invisible Line of Color

p. 77,   "One unidentified negro . . ." "28 Dead, 500 Hurt In Three-Day Race Riots in Chicago," *New York Times*, July 30, 1919, partners.nytimes.com/library/national/race/073019race-ra.html.

p. 78,   "HOG Butcher for the World . . ." "Carl Sandburg Poems - Chicago," http://carl-sandburg.com/chicago.htm.

p. 80,   "REDS TRY TO STIR . . ." "REDS TRY TO STIR NEGROES TO REVOLT: Widespread Propaganda on Foot Urging Them to Join I.W.W. and 'Left Wing Socialists,' " http://query.nytimes.com/mem/archive-free/pdf?res=9E07E0D71638E13ABC4051DFB1668382609EDE.

pp. 81-82,   "Headlines such as 'Negro . . ." "Chicago and Its Eight Reasons: Walter White Considers the Causes of the 1919 Chicago Race Riot," http://history-matters.gmu.edu/d/4978.

p. 85,   "It occurred at Wabash avenue . . ." "Ghastly Deeds of Race Rioters Told," The *Chicago Defender* Reports the Chicago Race Riot, 1919, http://history-matters.gmu.edu/d/4976.

p. 86,   "Frightened white men told me . . ." "Jazz Age Chicago - The Chicago Race Riot of 1919," http://chicago.urban-history.org/scrapbks/raceriot/rr_txt01.htm.

p. 87,   "Prior to 1915, Chicago . . ." "Chicago and Its Eight Reasons: Walter White Considers the Causes of the 1919 Chicago Race Riot," http://historymatters.gmu.edu/d/4978.

p. 87,   "Colored men saw their . . ." Walter White, "The Causes of the Chicago Race Riot," *The Crisis*, XVIII (October, 1919), 25.

p. 90,   "Eight months after the armistice . . ." Jan Voogd, *Race Riots and Resistance: The Red Summer of 1919* (New York: Peter Lang Publishing, 2008), 1.

CHAPTER 7: Tulsa, 1921: Blood on "Black Wall Street"

p. 91,   "Oh lawdy, me, . . ." James S. Hirsch, *Riot and Remembrance: America's Worst Race Riot and Its Legacy* (New York: Houghton Mifflin Company, 2002), 109.

p. 95,   "an orphan who works . . ." "Nab Negro Who Assaulted Girl in an Elevator," *Tulsa World*, http://www.tulsaworld.com/news/article.aspx?articleid=19210531_222_0_Anegro942113.

p. 101,   "Grand Jury Blames . . ." Alfred L. Brophy, *Reconstructing the Dreamland: The Tulsa Riot of 1921: Race, Reparations and Reconciliation* (Oxford University Press, New York: 2002), 74.

p. 101,   "had led (African Americans) . . ." Ibid, 75.

p. 104,   "We told these people . . ." Tim Madigan, *The Burning: Massacre, Destruction and the Tulsa Race Riot of 1921* (New York: Thomas Dunne Books, St. Martin's Press, 2001), 268.

CHAPTER 8: Detroit, 1943: Wrecking America's Arsenal

p. 105,   "Our . . . [race riot] in 1943 . . ." Elaine Latzman Moon, *Untold Tales, Unsung Heroes: An oral History of Detroit's African American Community, 1918-1967* (Detroit: Wayne State University Press, 1994), 83.

p. 112,   "We didn't know . . ." Alfred McLung Lee and Norman D. Humphrey, *Race Riot (Detroit, 1943)* (New York: Octagon Books, Inc., 1968), 38.

p. 116,   "a country torn by . . ." "The American Experience | Eleanor Roosevelt | People & Events | Detroit Race Riots 1943," PBS.org, http://www.pbs.org/wgbh/amex/eleanor/peopleevents/pande10.html.

p. 117,   "group of young Negro . . ." Lee and Humphrey, *Race Riot (Detroit, 1943)*, 69.

p. 117,   "ordinary law enforcement . . ." Ibid.

p. 118,   "I share your feeling . . ." "The American Experience | Eleanor Roosevelt | People & Events | Detroit Race Riots 1943," http://www.pbs.org/wgbh/amex/eleanor/peopleevents/pande10.

p. 118,   "the more we find . . ." "Meet The Press: Martin Luther King, Jr. on the Selma March," http://www.icue.com/portal/site/iCue/flatview/?cuecard=48756.

Bibliography

Barnes, Harper. *Never Been a Time: The 1917 Race Riot that Sparked the Civil Rights Movement.* New York: Walker & Company, 2008.

Bauerlein, Mark. *Negrophobia: A Race Riot in Atlanta, 1906.* San Francisco: Encounter Books, 2001.

Brophy, Alfred L. *Reconstructing the Dreamland : The Tulsa Riot of 1921.* Oxford: New York: Oxford University Press, 2002.

Cecelski, David S., and Timothy B. Tyson, eds. *Democracy Betrayed: The Wilmington Race Riot of 1898 and Its Legacy.* University of North Carolina Press: Chapel Hill, N.C., London, 1998.

Chicago Commission on Race Relations. *The Negro in Chicago; A Study of Race Relations and a Race Riot by the Chicago Commission on Race Relations.* Chicago, Ill.: University of Chicago Press, 1922.

Hirsch, James S. *Riot and Remembrance: The Tulsa Race War and Its Legacy.* Boston: Houghton Mifflin, 2002.

Hughes, Langston. *Fight for Freedom: The Story of the NAACP.* New York: Norton, 1962.

Jonas, Gilbert. *Freedom's Sword :The NAACP and the Struggle Against Racism in America, 1909-1969.* New York: Routledge, 2005.

Lee, Alfred McLung, and Norman D. Humphrey. *Race Riot (Detroit, 1943).* New York: Octagon Books, Inc., 1968.

Madigan, Tim. *The Burning: Massacre, Destruction and the Tulsa Race Riot of 1921.* New York: Thomas Dunne Books, St. Martin's Press, 2001.

Mixon, Gregory. *The Atlanta Riot: Race, Class and Violence in a New South City.* Gainesville, Florida: University Press of Florida, 2005.

Ovington, Mary White. *The Walls Came Tumbling Down.* New York: Harcourt, Brace, 1947.

Rudwick, Elliott M. *Race Riot at East St. Louis, July 2, 1917.* Carbondale: Southern Illinois University Press, 1964.

Sandburg, Carl. *The Chicago Race Riots, July, 1919.* New York: Harcourt, Brace & World, 1969.

Umfleet, LeRae Sikes. *A Day of Blood: The 1898 Wilmington Race Riot.* Raleigh, N.C.: North Carolina Office of Archives and History, in association with the African American Heritage Commission, 2009.

White, Walter Francis. *A Man Called White: The Autobiography of Walter White.* New York: Viking Press, 1948.

Web sites

http://www.tulsareparations.org/
Site of the Tulsa Reparations Coalition, with links to reparations efforts as well as histories of the riot.

http://docsouth.unc.edu/nc/kirk/kirk.html
A statement of facts about the Wilmington riot, by the Rev. J. Allen Kirk, with many details about the event and Kirk's own escape.

http://www.yale.edu/ynhti/curriculum/units/1979/2/79.02.04.x.html
A record of the "Negro Holocaust," including both urban riots and lynchings, by the Yale-New Haven Teachers Institute.

http://www.semp.us/publications/biot_reader.php?BiotID=414
The East St. Louis riot, by the Suburban Emergency Management Project.

http://library.thinkquest.org/2986/index.html
A student created web site on the Springfield riot, sponsored by the Oracle ThinkQuest Education Foundation.

http://www.pbs.org/wnet/jimcrow/stories_events_atlanta.html
The Atlanta riot, as part of the Public Broadcasting Service's series on Jim Crow times.

http://www.georgiaencyclopedia.org/nge/Home.jsp
The New Georgia Encyclopedia, with links on both the Atlanta riot and Rebecca Latimer Felton's remarks in the months leading to the Wilmington riot.

http://www.library.umass.edu/spcoll/digital/niagara.htm
Contains information on the Niagara Movement, with many primary source links.

http://chicago.urban-history.org/evt/evt01/evt0100.shtml
Covers the Chicago riot, as a dismal side of the exuberant "Jazz Age" of the 1920s.

http://apps.detnews.com/apps/history/index.php?id=185
Very detailed account of the Detroit riot by Vivian M. Baulch and Patricia Zacharias of the *Detroit News*.

Index

Photo Credits

All images used in this book that are not in the public domain are credited in the listing that follows.

Cover:	*The Detroit News* Archives
23:	NC Archives
25:	NC Archives
27:	NC Archives
29:	NC Archives
32-33:	NC Archives
44-45:	Courtesy of Library of Congress
58:	Courtesy of Library of Congress
68:	Courtesy of Tyson Blanquart
70:	Courtesy of Library of Congress
72:	Vintage Images / Alamy
75:	Courtesy of Library of Congress
93:	Courtesy of Library of Congress
94:	Courtesy of Beryl Ford Collection/Rotary Club of Tulsa, Tulsa City-County Library and Tulsa Historical Society
97:	Courtesy of Tulsa City-County Library
99:	Courtesy of Tulsa City-County Library
102-103:	Courtesy of Tulsa City-County Library
107:	Courtesy of Library of Congress
108:	Courtesy of Library of Congress
111:	Courtesy of Library of Congress
113:	*The Detroit News* Archives
114-115:	*The Detroit News* Archives
116:	*The Detroit News* Archives